P9-EMK-419

# DRUGS IN SPORTS

# Drugs in Sports

## Revised Edition

## Edward F. Dolan

Franklin Watts

New York     London     Toronto     Sydney

This book has been revised and updated from the previous edition, originally published under the title *Drugs in Sports* by Edward F. Dolan, Jr., published in 1986.

Library of Congress Cataloging-in-Publication

Dolan, Edward F., 1924-
Drugs in sports / by Edward F. Dolan. — Rev. ed.
p.    cm.
Includes bibliographical references (p.    ) and index.
Summary: Describes the widespread use of anabolic steroids, brake drugs, amphetamines, cocaine, and marijuana by athletes and discusses what the sports world has done to cope with drug abuse.
ISBN 0-531-11041-9
1. Doping in sports—Juvenile literature.    2. Athletes—Drug use—Juvenile literature.    [1. Athletes—Drug use.    2. Drug abuse.]
I. Title.
RC1230.D65   1992
362.29   dc20                                                    91-367-94 CIP AC

# CONTENTS

# DRUGS IN SPORTS

**Athletes under pressure to succeed have sometimes turned to drugs, looking for a "winning edge," or a way to escape the difficulties of sports competition.**

# INTRODUCTION
# DRUGS IN SPORTS

As we all know, today's world is suffering a major drug problem. Though drugs have been used since perhaps the dawn of human history, today's problem was born in the late 1950s and early 1960s. It was triggered by the stresses of the times and a number of other complex social factors. In the years since its birth, the problem has spread to all parts of the globe and to all walks of life, touching people of all ages.

Among the millions who have felt its touch are the vigorous people who are the subjects of this book—the world's athletes. Many have been caught up in the abuse of the so-called recreational drugs—cocaine, marijuana, and alcohol, to mention just three. Many have used legitimate medical drugs as training aids, but in ways and to extents that add up to a dangerous misuse. Such misuse can do—and has already done—extensive physical and psychological harm. The abuse and misuse have ruined careers and have severely damaged the reputation of sports throughout the world.

Of course, not all athletes are involved in the problem. There are competitors everywhere who want to have nothing to do with drugs. But the problem is there, and it has become so widespread over the years that it is now found among athletes at every level of competition—from world-class amateurs and highly paid professionals to high school and even junior high school performers.

It is an ugly and tragic problem that must be faced and discussed if it is somehow to be solved. And face it is what I plan to do in this book. We're going to look at all aspects of the problem—at the major drugs being misused and abused, at the harm they can do, at the athletes who risk that harm, and at the reasons why so many athletes feel driven to run that awful risk. Then we'll talk about how a troubled sports world is trying to end the misuse and abuse.

The problem is not only ugly and tragic but also complex, and so I have needed assistance in the preparation of this book. A word of appreciation is owed to everyone who has helped.

In particular, I wish to thank Anthony Maddalo, M.D., and Gilbert W. Gleim, Ph.D., of the Institute of Sports Medicine and Athletic Trauma at Lenox Hill Hospital in New York City for reviewing the original manuscript of this book to check that all the medical information in it is accurately stated.

And, for providing me with needed sports and drug research materials and for answering specific questions, I wish to thank the offices of the National Football League, the National League of Professional Baseball Clubs, the Major League Baseball Players Association, the Major League Player Relations Committee, the National Hockey League, and the Drug Enforcement Administration of the United States government. I also must thank the *Washington Post* newspaper for kindly permitting me to quote from articles on drug abuse in sports that appeared in its pages in 1979.

This book was first published in 1986. The aim of the revised edition is to add the information on drug use and abuse in sports that has come to light since 1986. The purpose of the revised edition remains the same as it was for the original book. It is to acquaint you with the dangerous drugs that are found in sports today so that you will understand their hazards. Armed with that knowledge and understanding, you may be able to make some contribution to ending their misuse and abuse. Perhaps you'll do so by talking with an athlete friend who is toying with them; perhaps by spreading the news among all your friends so that they, too, may take some kind of action; or perhaps—most important of all—by keeping these drugs out of your own life if you are an athlete.

Whatever action you take will be of great help. The misuse and abuse of drugs have become a health menace throughout the sports world. They are a menace that must be recognized and somehow eradicated if sports are to continue being what they have always been intended to be—healthful, enjoyable, and fair contests of physical prowess and skill.

—Edward F. Dolan
1992

# 1

# GOING FOR THE WINNING EDGE

---

☐ A pitcher with the San Diego Padres is suspended from professional baseball for one year on charges that he uses cocaine. He then receives a forty-five-day sentence for drug trafficking. At the end of his suspension he is given a tryout by the Chicago White Sox, only to be arrested again after police uncover a cache of marijuana and cocaine in his apartment.

☐ At the 1988 Olympic Games in Seoul, Korea, a track star flashes across the finish line after running the 100-meter (328-foot) dash in an amazing 9.79 seconds. His feat sets a world record and he is awarded a gold medal for the event. But the next day the International Olympic Committee strips him of his prize. Tests have revealed the presence in his system of a drug meant to increase his speed.

☐ The National Football League (NFL) suspends a Detroit Lions cornerback for life after he fails three medical tests for drug use. The lifetime ban may soon be rescinded, however. The athlete is told to wait a year before applying for readmittance to the NFL.

These three incidents made headlines in recent years—the first in 1987, the second in 1988, and the third in 1990. They are just a very few of many cases that have pointed up one of the saddest facts of our day and age. Just as drug abuse is a major problem in the world at large, so is it a major problem in a smaller world—a world of heroes who captivate us with their physical prowess and who serve as role models for young people everywhere—the world of sports.

We are shocked when we read stories exposing the misuse and abuse of drugs among athletes. But we must also keep two points in mind. First, there is nothing new about the use of drugs in athletics; as is true of society at large, drugs have played a role in the sports world for centuries. Second, there has been nothing sinister about much of their use in sports. Drugs have been widely used for legitimate medical purposes—for soothing tired and sore muscles, helping to heal injuries, and enabling competitors to perform up to par when beset by colds or the flu.

But, as in the three cases above—and it is here that we feel such deep shock—drugs *have* been abused as much in the sports world as in the larger world. Through the centuries, many of the men and women whose prowess and spirit of competitiveness we so much admire have taken them too frequently or in quantities too great for safety. Almost always those athletes have abused drugs for the purpose of keeping up with—or gaining some physical and perhaps unfair advantage over—their opponents. And many athletes have abused drugs for pleasure or as a temporary means of escaping the difficulties that life and sports competition have handed them.

Today, as is so true in the world at large, the presence of drugs in the sports world is greater than ever. The reasons for this are the same in both worlds. Modern science has developed more drugs—and for a wider variety of medical problems—than were ever dreamed of in earlier ages. Modern means of transportation and distribution have made these myriad drugs more readily available to greater numbers of people than ever before. Also, the pressures and strains of daily life seem especially sharp at present. The result: in increasing number and with increasing frequency, the two worlds have turned to the vast and readily available drug supply—sometimes for legitimate medical use, sometimes for misuse, and sometimes for outright abuse.

No one can deny that drugs, when wisely employed for medical purposes, are among the greatest boons ever given humankind. Drugs have done everything from relieving everyday aches and pains to eradicating some of the world's most feared diseases. Obviously, what is disrupting society and the sports world is not the legitimate medical use of drugs but their widespread misuse and outright abuse.

Not all athletes, of course, misuse or abuse drugs, or even take them at all. Nevertheless, so great has drug misuse and abuse become during recent years that it is now being called an international disaster. The problem has done physical and psychological damage to athletes of both sexes, of all nationalities, and at all levels of competition—from the highly paid professional to the beginning amateur. In some cases, it has even resulted in death. It has damaged the very nature of sports, twisting many of the world's best-loved games and events into anything but the healthful, exciting, and fair contests of skill and prowess that they were intended to be.

In this book, we are going to look at all aspects of this disaster.

## DRUGS AND SPORTS

The world's drugs can be divided into two basic types— the medical drugs and the drugs of abuse.

As we all know, the medical drugs available today are so plentiful as to seem countless. They vary in strength from mild, everyday medications that can be purchased over the counter in drugstores to highly potent and dangerous substances that require a doctor's prescription and careful medical supervision.

In sports the medical drugs are more likely to be misused than abused. Misuse can occur in any of several ways. For example, it often comes after an athlete obtains a legal prescription from a doctor to take a drug as an aid to his or her training. The athlete then wants more and more of the drug, all with the idea of continuing or increasing the drug's benefits. But the doctor, knowing the hazards of increased use, refuses to cooperate. Frustrated, the athlete turns to other sources—friends, fellow competitors, even the illegal drug market—for the needed supply. Free of medical supervision, the athlete almost always takes the drug with greater frequency and in larger and larger doses.

Another example: The athlete doesn't obtain a doctor's prescription in the first place, perhaps feeling that the physician will object to the drug as too dangerous for use. Or perhaps the athlete sees no need to see a doctor. The drug is being handed out by a friend, a fellow athlete, or a dealer.

No matter how the misuse occurs, it threatens damage to the body and mind because prolonged, heavy, and unsupervised doses of any potent drug increase the likelihood of dangerous effects. That damage can be terrible. Sometimes, the misuse is so great that it adds up to abuse.

And what of drugs of abuse? In sports as elsewhere, they are usually taken for pleasure or to escape the trials and pressures of life. The drugs of abuse are usually referred to as the "recreational drugs," a term that strikes many people as a sad commentary on modern life. How, they ask, can the obvious harmful effects of these drugs correspond at all with the idea of recreation and the healthful pleasures it is supposed to bring? Nevertheless, the term is widely used and accepted. Ranking highest among the popular recreational drugs of the 1980s and 1990s are cocaine and marijuana.

Within the sports world itself, various medical drugs have long been used. Like the drugs of the larger world, they, too, can be divided into two basic types.

First, there are the drugs intended for athletes who are unable to perform up to their usual standard. Perhaps the athlete is under some sort of heavy strain that interferes with effective performance. Or perhaps there has been an injury of some kind. Whatever the case, these drugs are meant to help the athlete return to normal or perform in spite of the problem.

Heading this type are such drugs as painkillers, tranquilizers, sedatives, and balms to reduce and soothe inflammations and muscle stiffness. Many are everyday drugs that do no harm when sensibly used.

The second type consists of drugs that *add* to the athlete's prowess. Their aim is to help the competitor perform beyond the level that he or she might reach without their aid. The athlete turns to these drugs in the hope that they will provide that all-important element in competition—the winning edge. Desired by all competitors—and desired *above all else* by some—the winning edge is the vital extra "something" that helps them to best the competition, outdo themselves, and become champions.

Just how do these drugs provide that edge? Some do the job by adding physical strength, some by instilling energy, and some by lifting the spirits and fostering strong feelings of self-confidence.

Because of such capabilities, the winning-edge drugs are extremely powerful and, consequently, dangerous substances. And also because of these capabilities, they are the medical drugs most misused in athletics today.

## GOING FOR
## THE EDGE

The desire for that winning edge which will help make you a champion is one of the main forces behind today's drug problem in sports. This desire has for centuries been a force behind the use of drugs in sports. It has long driven athletes to search for what can be called the perfect winning-edge drug. But, as doctors and many athletes are quick to point out, their search has been in vain. The perfect drug, the one that will give the edge without hurting the user, has yet to be found.

Their quest for that drug has caused the athletes to write an always strange and sometimes dangerous history. Over the years, they've tried everything from the most ineffective to the most lethal of concoctions.

For example, insofar as ineffective mixtures are concerned, many athletes of ancient times felt certain that strength and stamina came from drinking a liquid made of the crushed hooves of an Abyssinian ass. The hooves were boiled in oil along with some rose petals.

Not so useless, however, were the ashes from the burned leaves of South America's coca tree. The Inca Indians found that the ashes, when held in the mouth, somehow fired the body with great energy and made sleep unnecessary for several hours or even several days. The Incas used them when faced with tiring battles, hunts, and sporting competitions. Today, we know that the ashes contained the stimulant drug cocaine.

For generations, the Kaffir tribesmen of South Africa used a ceremonial drink called *dop* when engaged in war or athletics. Brewed of alcohol and cola, dop was supposed to provide extra energy and stamina. When the Boers settled in South Africa, they made the term a part of their language. However, they added an e to it and gave us the word that has come to mean all drugs: *dope*.

The mid-nineteenth century saw the beginnings of today's widespread development and manufacture of drugs. As the new drugs emerged from the laboratories of the day, many were tested by eager athletes in various nations. The French tried caffeine. The Belgians thought that ether would improve their performance; they managed to swallow the foul-tasting stuff by placing dabs of it on sugar cubes. A number of runners, on hearing that nitroglycerine causes the coronary arteries to dilate, felt that it could help them improve their speed. They reasoned that the widened arteries would allow more blood to reach the heart. In turn, the heart would beat faster. The result: a faster pace. Nothing of the sort happened. For their trouble the runners won nothing but violent headaches.

Racing cyclists in several European countries dreamed up an extra-energy recipe they called the "speedball." Stirred into it were two of nature's most deadly drugs— cocaine and heroin. In 1886 intake of the deadly pair claimed the life of a cyclist in a cross-country endurance event. His was the first drug-related death ever recorded in sports.

Tom Hicks of the United States was luckier. Minutes after winning the marathon event in the 1904 Olympics, he collapsed. When the runner finally regained consciousness, with the help of four doctors, it was found that he had fed himself something quite as dangerous as a speedball—a mixture of strychnine (a deadly poison in overdose) and brandy.

As we'll see in later chapters, the threat of damage and death has persisted to this day as athletes have continued to experiment with drugs that promise the winning edge by increasing strength, stamina, and confidence.

## TODAY'S WINNING-EDGE DRUGS

Today, in the winning-edge drug category, you'll find three especially potent and dangerous entries—the anabolic steroids, the amphetamines, and what are called "brake drugs."

The anabolic steroids are hormonal drugs that are thought to provide increased strength by building new body tissue. Some recent studies indicate that they do not build the tissue by themselves. Rather, it seems that they assist the building process by enabling athletes to do extended and rigorous workouts without suffering the muscle soreness that normally goes hand in hand with physical training.[1]

The amphetamines are chemical mixtures used for extra energy and confidence.

The brake drugs suppress—or put the "brakes" on— certain physical developments. Said by sports experts to be used principally in Eastern Europe, they serve to keep women gymnasts small and lithe.

There is a medical procedure that must also be placed in the same category as the drugs just mentioned, though it involves no drugs whatsover. It is called "blood boosting." Some doctors think it creates increased energy by pumping additional red cells into the athlete's system. It also helps by increasing the blood's oxygen-carrying capacity.

Even the so-called recreational drugs have come to be viewed as winning-edge drugs by many athletes. Cocaine is seen as advantageous by some because of the sudden thrust of energy and confidence that it provides. Some athletes turn to the depressant effects of marijuana to help them come down from the energy highs of cocaine and the amphetamines or to quiet the tensions of waiting for to-morrow's game.

In a book this size, it would be impossible to concentrate on every drug that has found a place in sports. There will be no need to mention the mildest of the lotions and balms that ease the pains of injury and stress. Nor will we talk about the various drugs that are used by just a few athletes. Among such drugs are the relaxants manufactured under such brand names as Valium and Raudixin. They are often a help to archers, golfers, and firearms marksmen who wish to steady their hands.

Rather, our attention in the coming chapters will go to the drugs that are misused or abused by the greatest number of athletes—drugs that also happen to do the greatest harm because of their potency. In turn, we'll look at the medical drugs athletes eagerly seek in the hope of gaining that all-important winning edge: (1) the anabolic steroids, (2) the amphetamines, and (3) the brake drugs. Then we'll turn to the nondrug procedure, blood boosting, and go from there to the abuse of today's chief recreational drugs—cocaine and marijuana.

Throughout the book, we'll have five questions upper-most in mind:

**1.** What do these drugs contain?
**2.** How do they work on the body and mind?
**3.** What physical and psychological harms can they do?
**4.** Why do many athletes turn to these drugs when their dangers are so well known?
**5.** What is the sports world doing to curb or halt to-day's widespread misuse and abuse of drugs?

Let's consider these questions first as they relate to the group of drugs whose misuse is said to have reached epidemic proportions worldwide. The U.S. government's Federal Drug Administration reports that these drugs can induce some seventy short- and long-term dangerous side effects.[2] They are the anabolic steroids.

# 2

# ANABOLIC STEROIDS: A HEALTH MENACE

☐ The California bodybuilder was delighted. In just a few months, he had added 30 pounds (13.6 kg) to his slender but muscular frame. But then he suddenly doubled over with severe abdominal cramps. On examining him, doctors found a cancerous tumor clinging to his liver. The tumor weighed almost 4 pounds (1.8 kg). To save the young man's life, surgeons had to remove two-thirds of his liver.[1]

☐ At age twenty-two, the athlete was agile and slim. Her sport was basketball. She was practicing and exercising daily in the hope of making the women's team in the 1984 Olympics. Over a period of several months, she was appalled to see her muscles beginning to bulge too much. She heard her voice grow deeper as time went by. A darkish stain broke out on her upper lip. It was the beginnings of a mustache. Horrified, the young woman felt that she was turning into a man.

☐ Larry Pacifico is a world-class powerlifter. He holds a record nine consecutive world titles in his sport, won between 1971 and 1979. In 1981, at age thirty-five, Pacifico underwent surgery on his elbow. After the operation, while yet in the hospital recovery room, he was struck with a heart attack. An examination showed that two of the arteries to his heart had become 70 percent blocked. A third artery was 99.9 percent blocked. Pacifico was lucky he did not die. An operation helped to save his life.

These three athletes competed in different sports. Each trained in his or her own way. But they had one thing in common: each had taken some form of the drugs known as anabolic steroids.

The three were not drug abusers. They had not been looking for the "kicks," "highs," and escapes from reality to be found in the recreational drugs. Rather, they had turned to the anabolic steroids for help. They knew them to be substances with an amazing ability—the ability to help build new body tissue quickly. New body tissue would bring increased strength. In the increased strength, the trio hoped to find that winning edge—that invaluable extra something that would help them best all the competition.

But the drugs seem to have backfired. Since the use of steroids was the one thing that the three athletes had in common, it struck everyone that the steroids must have been behind all the trouble. The hospital doctors blamed them for the giant tumor attached to the young bodybuilder's liver. The woman basketball star was sure they were making her look more and more like a man. Larry Pacifico was equally certain that they had caused the blockage of his arteries.

The three cases are frightening. But they are far from unusual. The anabolic steroids were first developed in Europe in the 1930s. They were intended and initially used for medical purposes only. Later, a few athletes in search of that all-important winning edge began to experiment with them. Since then, steroid use in sports has fanned out to all parts of the world. With that widespread use, the steroids have proven to be not only amazing body builders but also drugs that can do terrible physical and psychological damage. A steadily increasing number of sports and medical authorities are coming to regard their spread as a worldwide health menace.

## EARLY STEROID USE

When they were first developed, the anabolic steroids were thought by doctors to be miracle drugs. Their ability to help build new body tissue made them superb medications for patients recovering from starvation and for the victims of severe injury; their first widespread application came at the end of World War II, when they were used to help rebuild the undernourished and broken bodies of the people who had survived the horrors of the Nazi concentration camps.[2] Anabolic steroids also did much to prevent the withering of muscle tissue in patients forced to remain inactive for long periods after surgery. In addition, research found that they could be helpful to girls suffering the delayed arrival of puberty. Today, the steroids continue to serve these medical purposes.

Because of their marvelous body-building capabilities, the steroids could not long escape the eye of the sports world. Athletic experimentation with them was under way by the mid-1950s and may have begun several years earlier. Exact dates are not available because the first sports use took place in countries behind the Communist Iron Curtain. It was kept a secret from the Western world. Soon, however, the whispered word was leaking out that here were drugs that could increase strength and give their users a real edge.

The word seemed true. Russian weight lifters were among the first to use the steroids. Aided by the drugs and state-sponsored training programs that provided ample hours for workouts, the lifters developed into massive and powerful athletes. The result: they dominated their sport worldwide for years.

Soon, however, the steroids began to be unmasked as anything but helpful to athletes. Ever since the drugs had first appeared, research into their effects on the body had been conducted on animals and humans. As yet, the research was far from complete (it is still incomplete as you read this book), but the studies indicated that the steroids were dangerous. Especially if not taken under strict medical supervision, they could harm a user in various ugly ways— and, they seemed able to kill.

## THE PROBLEM SPREADS

Yet, despite all the frightening indications, a steadily growing number of athletes turned to the anabolic steroids over the years, sometimes with medical supervision and sometimes with no supervision whatsoever as they tried them on their own. From this experimentation behind the Iron Curtain, steroid use spread to the rest of Europe and then to western hemisphere countries, among them the United States and Canada. The earliest use appears to have been limited mainly to weight lifters and powerlifters. Since then, though it must always be stressed that most athletes are not users, the steroids have found their way into a wide variety of sports, including track, football, and basketball. In these sports the drugs are used not only for increased strength but also for the extra speed and agility that increased strength can bring.

For a number of years, use was pretty much limited to the elite of the sports world—to competitors striving for national and international titles. Many sports meets have long employed saliva and urine tests to ensure that the competitors neither jeopardize their health nor gain an unfair advantage by taking certain drugs. Failure to pass the tests results in disqualification from the meet. These tests have revealed some of the world's finest athletes to be steroid users.

There are numerous examples of world-class athletes having tested positive for steroid use. In the late 1970s, two great women track-and-field stars—East Germany's Ilona Slupianek and Russia's Nadezhda Tkachenko—were made to surrender the medals they had won in international competition. Slupianek lost the gold medal she had taken in the shot put at the 1977 European Cup meet, while Tkachenko had to surrender the gold medal for the pentathlon in the 1978 European Championships. At about the same time, Russian swimmer Viktor Kuznetsov lost his bronze medal won for the 100-meter (328-foot) backstroke at the West Berlin swimming championships. And discus thrower Markku Tuokko of Finland had to give up his gold medal in the 1977 European Cup.

More recently, the International Weight Lifting Feder-

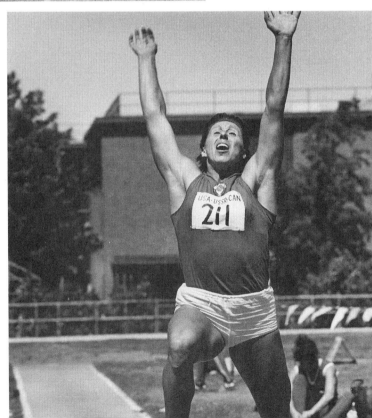

ation disqualified nine steroid users during a mid-1980s world championship meet held in Ohio. Even worse, fifteen world-class competitors in lifting and track and field were expelled from the 1983 Pan American Games at Caracas, Venezuela, when steroids were detected in their systems. Surrendered by the fifteen were twenty-three medals.

The Ohio and Venezuela disqualifications did more than show that steroids were being used by many top-flight athletes. They also left no doubt as to how far steroid use had spread in the world. Disqualified at Ohio and Caracas were competitors representing fourteen nations—Argentina, Canada, Chile, Colombia, Cuba, the Dominican Republic, Hungary, Japan, Nicaragua, Poland, Puerto Rico, the Soviet Union, the United States, and Venezuela.

What is probably the best-known disqualification for steroid use came during the 1988 Summer Olympic Games at Seoul, Korea, when the sprinter Ben Johnson was disqualified and stripped of his gold medal after winning the 100-meter dash in record-breaking time.

## THE BEN JOHNSON SCANDAL

At the time Ben Johnson came to Seoul, the ban against the use of steroids by Olympic competitors was fifteen years old.[3] The International Olympic Committee (IOC) had added them to the list of forbidden drugs in 1973, saying that they were physically dangerous and, because they provided such a "winning edge," unfair. The Committee announced that the discovery of the drug in an athlete's system would result in disqualification and the loss of any medals won. Earlier, at the Mexico City Games in 1968, the IOC had banned the use of the energy-generating amphetamines and then had

**Shot put star Ilona Schoknecht and pentathlon champion Nadezhda Tkachenko both lost medals after testing positive for steroid use in the 1970s.**

given increasing attention to the steroids in the next years as their widespread use became more and more known.

The twenty-seven-year-old Johnson competed in the Seoul Games as a member of the Canadian team. He had been born in Jamaica but had moved from there to the city of Toronto in 1976. In Canada, his athletic abilities had soon won everyone's respect. They were abilities that eventually lifted him to stardom in world-class track meets. In 1987 he set the world's record of 9.83 seconds for the 100-meter dash at an international competition in Rome.

Hailed as "the world's fastest human" after his Rome triumph, the sprinter proceeded to break his own record in the 100-meter event at Seoul, shaving several fractions of a second off his time and winning the event's gold medal when he sprinted across the finish line in an astonishing 9.79 seconds. Close behind him in second place, posting a run of 9.92 seconds, came Carl Lewis of the United States. Finishing in third and fourth places respectively were Great Britain's Linford Christie and America's Calvin Smith.

While the watching world was applauding his victory, Johnson underwent a urine test immediately after the race. When the test proved positive, indicating the presence of a forbidden drug in his system, he was tested again twenty-four hours later. (Giving a second test is a routine IOC procedure whenever a first test shows up positive.) On receiving the final test results, the IOC shocked the world with the announcement that Johnson was being disqualified and stripped of his gold medal. The test had detected the presence of stanozolol, an anabolic steroid, in his system. Stanozolol is a synthetic form of the male hormone, testosterone.

The IOC then awarded the 100-meter gold medal to runner-up Carl Lewis. The silver went to Linford Christie, and the bronze to Calvin Smith. Johnson became the seventh athlete and the third gold medalist to be disqualified at Seoul under the IOC's drug-testing program. (IOC officials had predicted that perhaps fifteen of all the competitors at the Games would fail the tests. Actually, only ten of the 13,674 participating athletes from 161 nations were disqualified for using banned substances.)

**The Canadian sprinter Ben Johnson,
seen here leading the field, lost
his Olympic gold medal when tests
showed an anabolic steroid
in his system.**

The other deposed gold medalists were two Bulgarian weight lifters, who were found to have the banned drug furosemide in their systems. Upon the disqualification of the pair, the entire Bulgarian weight-lifting team withdrew from the competition. Furosemide is a diuretic, meaning that it induces increased urination. As such, it can be used for quick weight loss to keep athletes within the weight class in which they compete. It can also be used to mask the presence of other drugs in the athlete's system by diluting the urine samples.

Johnson returned to Canada in disgrace. His track exploits had made him a hero to the entire country, but now, though many Canadians were sympathetic to his plight, he was widely criticized for "cheating" in his races. People throughout Canada and the world felt that he had become an international track star not through his natural abilities and long hours of training but through the help of a winning-edge drug.

The fact that stanozolol, and not some other steroid, was found in his system added to the feeling that he had been cheating. It was known that many athletes employed the substance because, unlike other steroids, it leaves the body quickly and had always been impossible to detect in drug testing. But, two years before the Seoul Games, a test had been devised to reveal its presence. Johnson was said to have been unaware of the new test and had been caught by it.

There was also a mystery surrounding the presence of the drug in his system. Johnson's manager, Larry Heidebrecht, claimed that the sprinter was innocent of taking stanozolol. He said it must have been slipped to Johnson without his knowledge at some point during the track competitions so that it would show up in the post-race tests and lead to a disqualification. Heidebrecht told the press that someone—an official or a volunteer worker—had given Johnson a bottle of the "energy drink" Gatorade to take either before the semifinal or final 100-meter dash (Heidebrecht could not recall which), and that Johnson had drunk it. The manager went on to say that later, Johnson's doctor had noticed a thickish yellow substance in the bottom of the bottle, thought its odor peculiar, and rinsed the bottle out.

The IOC disagreed with the claim that Johnson had been given "spiked" Gatorade. The Committee announced that the analysis of Johnson's urine sample had shown that his testosterone level was 15 percent above normal. That level was consistent with long-term steroid use rather than with a single instance of a sabotaged drink.

Whether he was unjustly harmed by an unknown enemy before his Seoul races or guilty of deliberately using a steroid to achieve a winning edge, Johnson was banished from track competition for more than two years. He returned in January 1991, when he competed in the Hamilton Spectator Indoor Games in the Canadian province of Ontario. Clocked at 5.77 seconds, he placed second in the first 50-meter (164-foot) race of his career. His time was 0.16 second off the world indoor mark for the distance. Johnson's performance caused sports reporters to write that he now might be able to run as well as before, this time without the aid of steroids.

## EPIDEMIC PROPORTIONS

Today, steroid use is no longer limited to the elite of the sports world. It has spread to athletes of all ages at all levels of competition—to any athlete who wants to win at any and all costs. Studies and news reports show that today's users range from world-class amateurs and highly paid professionals to college, high school, and even junior high school athletes.

While it must always be stressed that many athletes do not take steroids—or any drug whatsoever—steroid use has now, in the words of Dr. Clayton Thomas of the Olympic Sports Medicine Council, reached international epidemic proportions.

No one can say exactly how many athletes have turned to steroids in recent years. But a number of recent statements by sports figures can give us an idea of just how widespread the use must be.

For example, Dr. James Wright, a well-known authority

in sports medicine, was reported in a 1982 issue of *Sports Illustrated* as saying that as much as 70 to 80 percent of the steroids in the United States are not being used for their original purpose of healing illness and injury. Rather, they are being taken by athletes to increase their prowess.

Next, *Science* magazine in 1988 reported Dr. David L. Black's belief that there are at least 1 million people taking steroids in the United States. Dr. Black is the director of the Athletic Drug Testing Laboratory at Vanderbilt University in Nashville, Tennessee; the laboratory conducts steroid testing for the National Football League and a number of college teams. He told *Science* that, in international meets, between 1 and 2 percent of the competitors test positive for the steroids. From 7 to 8 percent of professional football players test positive. Five percent test positive in college athletics.[4]

A senior track-and-field coach at Canada's Simon Fraser University recently informed the press that he feels the use of the drugs is so widespread in sports that, whenever he sees a superior performance by an athlete, he automatically asks himself what the competitor is "on."[5]

The statements of some top-notch athletes may reveal the extent of steroid use even more. A track-and-field star of the 1980 Olympics says that many athletes would have dropped out of the Games had the word gone around that some new test had been developed that could expose anyone who had ever used the drug. A professional football player believes that anyone who graduated from college and entered the professional ranks in the early to mid-1980s was using steroids. A college powerlifter flatly admits that every lifter of his acquaintance is a user. A California letterman in several high school sports says that one of his coaches put him on steroids.

In the early days of steroid use, some coaches and trainers gave their athletes steroids without a doctor's advice and supervision because they did not understand how harmful the drugs could be. Most stopped the practice when the steroid hazards became better known. Today, the coaches and trainers who continue to obtain and give the steroids on their own are thought to be relatively few in number and are roundly criticized by their more sensible colleagues. A principal charge leveled against them is that they are so eager for victory or a championship that they will risk the health of their athletes to achieve it. Such coaches and trainers are rarely discovered, tried, and convicted.

One of the most tragic aspects of the steroid epidemic is pointed out by Dr. Herbert A. Haupt, an orthopedic surgeon in St. Louis, Missouri. He believes the greatest steroid abuse is to be found not in sports competition but in local gyms and health clubs. There, he contends, countless young men turn to the steroids because they suffer from low self-esteem and wish to build it through developing their bodies to muscleman proportions. They then become psychologically dependent on the drugs to maintain their all-important physical appearance and to continue bolstering their self-esteem. Dr. Haupt brands this kind of behavior as self-destructive.[6]

Possibly the greatest steroid tragedy of all has been the spread of the drug among younger competitors such as the above-mentioned California letterman—athletes at the high school and junior high school level. In the late 1980s a national study by Pennsylvania Sate University revealed that some 7 percent of U.S. senior high school boys have at least experimented with the steroids.[7] This finding was followed in 1990 by the results of a study conducted by the U.S. Department of Health and Human Services. The Department estimated that some 250,000 of the nation's adolescents, both male and female, are using or have used the steroid drugs. The Department further estimated that from 5 to 10 percent of boys and from 0.2 to 0.5 percent of girls are involved in steroid usage.[8]

Fifty-five young users were interviewed as part of the Health and Human Services study. What they said alarmed many doctors and sports authorities. For example, 93 percent said they felt they had made a good decision in turning to the drugs, with 87 percent then stating that they would reach the same decision today "without hesitation." Upwards of 80 percent believed that the steroids had made them bigger, stronger, better-looking, and, as a result, more popular among their peers. About 85 percent reported that their friends had influenced them to begin taking the drugs. Eighty-two percent did not believe the medical claims about the harms that the steroids can do to the body.[9]

Surveys conducted with young Americans ten to fourteen years old have given equally disturbing results. Despite the warnings in the press and in school programs of the possible harmful effects of the steroids, 43 percent of the youngsters interviewed in one such survey felt that no damage will be done if the user is careful. Forty-five percent expressed the belief that steroids do improve athletic skills, while 55 percent said that the drugs alone will build muscle size and strength. Some 15 percent admitted they might turn to the steroids in the future. A whopping 88 percent were convinced that Olympic competitors use steroids.[10]

*JAMA: The Journal of the American Medical Association* sees the outlooks expressed in the surveys and the Health and Human Services study as dangerous because they indicate that young people are casual and accepting in their attitudes about the use of steroids. In a 1990 editorial, *JAMA* contended that the youngsters' outlooks are particularly upsetting because so little is as yet known about what the drugs can do to a body still in its formative stages. *JAMA* speculated that future research may well show that steroids are more harmful to the very young than to older athletes, whose hormonal and bone development is complete. The editorial ended with a call for increased and more-innovative educational programs to acquaint young people with the steroid dangers and to get them to act on the knowledge they receive.[11]

The epidemic of steroid use is seen by many medical and sports authorities as one of the greatest menaces in the current drug problem because the research into the steroids continues to make their awful dangers clearer and clearer. We will be looking more closely at those dangers in a few pages. In the meantime, we need to know some basic facts about the steroids themselves.

## WHAT ARE
## ANABOLIC
## STEROIDS?

The answer to this question begins when we define each word in the term "anabolic steroid." "Anabolic" means the ability to promote body growth and repair body tissue. It comes from the Greek word *anabolikos*, meaning "constructive." "Steroid" refers to a number of compounds of a certain chemical nature.

The basic chemicals that make up the steroid compounds are the body substances called *hormones*. These hormones may be given to an individual in their natural state. They may be given as *synthetics*, meaning that their natural structure has been altered in the laboratory to make them better able to perform certain medical tasks. There are also steroids in which hormones are not actually present. Such steroids are composed of chemicals that, when mixed together, achieve the same results as the hormones.

Different kinds of hormones can be used in steroids. One kind, for example, comes from the adrenal glands, which are located just above the kidneys and secrete various needed body chemicals. Another kind is progesterone, a hormone found in females. Still another is testosterone, which is found principally in males. Some steroids are made of combinations of different hormones.

In sum, then, anabolic steroids are drugs that come from hormones (or from combinations of chemicals that achieve the same results as the hormones) and that prompt the growth of healthy body tissue. They are manufactured today in a number of forms—as powders and tablets to be taken orally, and as liquids to be injected into the muscles.

Many types of steroids have been produced through the years to treat various illnesses and disorders. One of the best known of all is cortisone, a medication used in the treatment of problems ranging from rheumatoid arthritis and rheumatic fever to a number of allergic conditions. Cortisone is one of the many hormones made by the adrenal glands.

## TESTOSTERONE STEROIDS

One last point must be stressed. In the main, of all the different steroids available today, the ones taken by athletes contain testosterone or chemicals that act as the hormone does. As previously mentioned, testosterone is found in men and is produced in the testicles. It is also found in women, but in much smaller amounts. In the coming pages, we'll be talking almost always about the steroids that spring from this particular hormone. Today, more than 120 testosterone steroids are marketed throughout the world. They are manufactured under a variety of brand names.

And now it's time to talk in detail of the potential dangers of steroids—dangers to both the body and the mind.

# 3

# ANABOLIC STEROIDS: BROKEN BODIES, TROUBLED MINDS

The anabolic steroids can be called "dual personality" drugs. On the one hand, they are able to do fine medical work. But, on the other, especially if carelessly used, they can have harmful side effects, or results other than those intended. The steroids resemble many another valuable medical drug in their dual personality. One example is the splendid painkiller, morphine. It must always be handled with extreme caution because it has addictive side effects that can enslave a patient.

Despite their dangers, the steroids can be obtained over the counter in some countries—that is, they can be bought at drugstores or markets by anyone, just as if they were aspirin or a cough remedy. In other nations, where the drug-control laws are stricter, the potent side effects are recognized and the steroids can be obtained only with a doctor's prescription. The United States is one of the countries requiring a doctor's prescription.

## DOCTORS AND STEROIDS

Along with doctors elsewhere in the world, physicians in the United States who deal with athletes differ in their views of steroid consumption. Some will not prescribe the drugs at all for sports use, regarding them as too dangerous to be given to perfectly healthy individuals. Some refuse prescriptions on the grounds that the swallowing of some pills to gain a winning edge adds up to cheating. And some see them as unnecessary for top athletic performance. Along with all the athletes, coaches, and trainers who oppose any sort of drug use, they feel that good diet, healthful living habits, and steady training are the elements best able to ensure a sparkling performance.

But other physicians are willing to prescribe the steroids for adult athletes and do so for a variety of reasons. Some consider the drugs safe when administered under medical supervision—a supervision that carefully regulates the dosages and then quickly adjusts them or ends the use at the first sign of trouble.

Others don't like the steroids but understand that many an eager competitor will seek them from other sources if refused a prescription. Those sources are all too many and all too easy to reach on today's worldwide drug scene— friends, fellow athletes, trainers and coaches, the black market, and drugstores in those countries where the steroids can be legally purchased over the counter. Understanding all this, the doctors reluctantly go ahead and authorize the drug's use rather than let the athletes risk taking it on their own. At the least, they are then able to supervise its administration and watch for trouble.

Still other doctors recognize the possible serious harmful side effects, but say that everyone does not necessarily suffer from them. They point out that even aspirin, one of the least dangerous of all drugs, can do damage. But millions of people take aspirin safely because its harmful side effects are generally slight and experienced by relatively few users, while its painkilling capabilities are great. These physicians feel much the same way about steroid use under medical supervision. They feel that the use may well not harm most athletes because they are in such fine physical shape and that it can be stopped if harmful side effects manifest themselves. They also feel that the body-building benefits to be achieved outweigh the risks involved.

Who has the right idea here? The doctor who refuses to prescribe the steroids, or the doctor who writes a prescription. There is no final answer—and may never be. It is all a matter of medical opinion and judgment on the part of the individual physicians.

But one point is certain. Research and the experience of users leave no doubt that the greatest harm has been done when athletes have obtained the steroids on their own and used them without medical supervision.

What has happened to these athletes? Almost invariably, not knowing what amounts can be taken with reasonable safety, the athletes have downed far too much of the drug, perhaps right from the start. And in keeping with the general points made about misuse in Chapter One, they have almost invariably increased the dosages as they've gone along. They've told themselves that the continuing use and the increased dosages would give greater benefits. Some doctors say that many athletes take between 10 and 100 times the normal steroid doses. Other physicians estimate even higher overdoses: between 100 and 1,000 times the normal dosages.[1]

Because the steroids are so potent, prolonged use of small amounts can be dangerous. Extended use of heavy amounts may prove to be lethal. What we'll see in the next pages is the great harm that prolonged use—especially prolonged heavy use—has caused.

Basically, but in very complicated ways, the anabolic steroids cause this harm by upsetting the body's chemistry and hormonal balance. The upset results from jamming the system with excess testosterone (or, in those compounds that do not actually contain testosterone, with chemicals that act like it). The upset causes the same kinds of damage in both males and females. But there are also special harms done to women alone, and special harms just for men. Let's look at these various damages in turn.

## HAZARDS FOR BOTH MEN AND WOMEN

To begin, some doctors suspect that anabolic steroids bring on—or help to bring on—heart attacks by causing the arteries to harden and thicken. The result is arteriosclerosis, the condition that almost killed Larry Pacifico. It has also been found that the steroids prompt the body to retain too much water. This retention leads to a rising blood pressure that, if left unattended, can lead to a heart attack or stroke. A stroke occurs when a blood vessel bursts in the brain.

The noted researcher in anabolic steroids, Bob Goldman, explains how the steroids cause the body to retain water in dangerous amounts. In his book *Death in the Locker Room* (written with Patricia Bush and Ronald Klatz), Goldman points to the basic fact that our bodies contain a number of chemicals, among them chlorine, sodium, potassium, and nitrogen. A certain amount of water is needed to balance these chemicals. The steroids cause the body to retain too much nitrogen. To balance things out, the body begins to retain more water. A strain is put on the blood vessels because they must now pump increased amounts of fluid through the system. Up goes the blood pressure. In time the strain proves too great—the heart gives out or a blood vessel snaps in the brain.

And there is an allied problem. The increased amount of fluid causes the body to expand with what athletes have come to call "steroid bloat." They try to right things by taking diuretics, which are medications that empty the fluid by causing excessive urination. The diuretics may help to end the bloating, but in at least one instance their use has ended in tragedy.

Recently, a young California weight lifter died of a heart attack after using steroids for some months. When doctors conducted a postmortem on his body, they found that he had also been taking diuretics in large dosages. The diuretics induced a urination so heavy that it purged his system of electrolytes. These are chemicals (a chief one is potassium) that assist in regulating the heartbeat. Once they were too far reduced, his heart became unable to endure the resulting irregularity.

Current research (backed by user experiences) strongly indicates that steroids can either cause or help to cause cancerous tumors in the liver and possibly in the kidneys. As a tragic case in point here, you'll recall the young California bodybuilder who had to have two-thirds of his cancerous liver removed.

The steroids are also suspected of bringing on liver and kidney failure. In *Death in the Locker Room*, Bob Goldman points to these suspicions by telling the story of another bodybuilder—a dark-haired, twenty-three-year-old who looked the picture of glowing health with his rippling muscles and broad shoulders. Suddenly, however, the young man began to show the signs of liver disease: his skin turned yellow; a severe itch plagued his entire body. He became so ill one night that his parents rushed him to the hospital, where he was diagnosed as suffering from liver-kidney failure. He died four days later.

Though supposed to develop and strengthen muscle tissue, the steroids seem just as capable of destroying it. The destruction seems especially prevalent among weight lifters. Eric Hoffman, long a major figure in United States lifting, wrote of the problem in an article published by *Sports Illustrated* magazine in 1982.

Hoffman said that muscle and tendon injuries were rare in his sport until lifters began taking steroids. Now, such injuries are commonplace, with the biceps (in the arm) and the quadriceps (at the front of the thigh) being the muscles most frequently harmed. Hoffman reported that scores of lifters have suffered the frightening experience of seeing their biceps muscle roll up the arm "like a windowshade" after the tendon holding it to the bone broke away. Others have collapsed during training or competition when the tendons holding their quadriceps in place gave way.

In young athletes who have not yet reached their full height, the steroids are accused of causing acne (doing the same thing in some adults) and halting bone growth.

All types of damage caused by steroids are usually not reversible—meaning that the damage will not disappear when usage is stopped—when the steroids have been taken heavily for prolonged periods. Some types of damage are reversible among light or infrequent steroid users.

Injuries due to a steroid habit are a particular danger during training sessions, because it is believed that the drug does not build new muscle tissue solely by itself.[2] Rather, as you'll recall from Chapter One, it seems to help build the tissue by enabling the athlete to train harder and longer without having to endure the muscle soreness that goes hand in hand with workouts. Unfortunately—especially for those competitors who are dedicated to mastering their sport—the extended and vigorous training sessions can easily lead to overtraining and injury. What happens is simply that the trainees unwisely push themselves beyond the limits of the body's natural defenses and then suffer when something inside breaks down. Some of the above-mentioned bicep and quadricep injuries may have been caused by unwise overtraining.

Another example of a training mishap involves Ben Johnson. He sustained a painful hamstring injury, thought to have been caused by his steroid intake, during the months of training prior to the 1988 Olympic Games. Since the steroids are known to accelerate the healing process, it is also thought that Johnson added to his woes by taking them to help end his hamstring problem.

Many doctors point to yet another possible danger so far as injury is concerned. Most athletes have a "sixth sense" that tells them when they have worked enough for the day. But the steroids, along with helping the trainee to avoid the pain of muscle soreness (or perhaps because of the absence of pain), seem to hand out an excess of energy and confidence. That excess may work to deaden the athlete's all-important "sixth sense."

## SPECIAL HAZARDS FOR WOMEN

To understand the special hazards for women, we have to add a new term to the definition of anabolic steroids containing testosterone or chemicals that act like testosterone. They are not only body-building and tissue-repairing drugs, but also *androgenic* drugs. An androgenic subtance—also called an *androgen*—is one that promotes the signs of masculinity. It brings on the development of the male sex organs and is responsible for the man's beard, body hair, and deep voice. It is likewise responsible for the male's heavy muscle mass. In the main, the steroids prompt this building of weight and muscle mass by increasing the body's ability to absorb protein.

Obviously, these steroids promote the signs of masculinity because, though some testosterone is naturally produced in females, it is a male hormone.

In women, the small amount of testosterone is kept in balance with the *estrogens*, the hormones that give the woman her feminine characteristics and regulate her reproductive cycle. Additional amounts of testosterone rapidly destroy this balance, with the result that she begins to show a series of male characteristics.

The woman sees the gentle curves of her body begin to vanish, to be replaced by hard and bulging masses of muscle. She gains weight. Her voice deepens, and her skin roughens. A mustache appears, and baldness may occur.

Men also experience the roughening of the skin and the growth of excess hair. The hair, looking as if it better belongs to King Kong, appears in dark splashes on various parts of the body.

The changes that occur in a woman may not be reversible once well started. Further, their onset cannot be prevented should the woman try to hold them off or counterbalance them by using drugs containing the female hormone, estrogen. In fact, studies indicate that women face an increased danger of certain cancers when using steroids while taking birth control pills. These contraceptives all contain estrogen.

The woman is not alone in running the risk of all the changes. Her unborn children are also in danger. In *Death in the Locker Room*, Bob Goldman writes that the female baby in the uterus of a woman taking steroids will develop such male traits as extra hair. Also, many doctors suspect that steroid use may lead the women to give birth to deformed and handicapped children.

This suspicion has yet to be confirmed through research. But it is strong enough to have caused a number of women competitors to fear having children. As one California athlete has said, "I really want to have children. But I'm afraid to. I just don't know how normal they would be. The whole thing scares me to death."

In addition to all these dangers, women run an increased risk of breast cancer.

## SPECIAL HAZARDS FOR MEN

Many male athletes who use steroids have experienced a shrinking (called *atrophy*) of the testicles. In a number of cases, this condition has been accompanied by a falling sperm count, a lessening of sexual desire, and infertility (the inability to father a child). Stanozolol, the steroid found in Ben Johnson's system at the Seoul Games, can do this sort of harm. It is known to do irreversible damage to the testicles and cause impotence (the inability to have sexual intercourse) and infertility. (In women it can result in serious skin problems, irregularities in menstruation, and the outbreak of such male characteristics as facial hair.) Stanozolol, as you'll recall from the Johnson story, is a synthetic version of the male hormone, testosterone.[3]

Some male athletes have suffered an enlargement of the prostate gland (the gland that produces the fluid in which the male sperm resides). The condition is a painful one that is not usually found in men under age fifty. Quite often the male user develops breasts like those of a woman.

Steroid use may also increase the risk of cancer. In mid-1991, the press reported a tragic case in point. At age forty-one, Lyle Alzado, an outstanding player for fourteen years with the National Football League, was found to have inoperable brain cancer. Doctors told him they believed the cancer was a direct result of his use of anabolic steroids. In a television interview he said he had used the drugs in various forms throughout his NFL career.[4]

## HAZARDS TO THE MIND

Research into the manner in which the steroids affect the user's personality is showing that they act in much the same way as the amphetamine drugs. Amphetamines are chemical mixtures that erase fatigue, fill the user with energy, and enable him or her to perform tirelessly for long hours. When the drugs wear off, the user enters a period of exhaustion that is often accompanied by feelings of deep depression. Extended use of the amphetamines, as we'll see in a later chapter, can induce chronic depression, irrational behavior, and hallucinations.

Athletes who have taken steroids say that, along with providing gains in strength, the drugs made them feel energetic, tough, and confident. They became more aggressive in both training and competition, wanting even more than before to be champion performers. So far as many athletes are concerned, these feelings are all to the good. As they see it, the feelings have added to that winning edge.

But if this is indeed the case, the steroids have at the same time exacted a terrible psychological price. Users have felt—and their friends have seen—wild swings in mood. In moments, the athletes have gone flashing from highs of confidence and happiness to lows of depression and anger. Many have found themselves sleeping restlessly. Some of the most easygoing of individuals have watched their natural sense of competitiveness turn into a sharp, and even dangerous, hostility toward their opponents in meets and games.

A recent issue of *Sports Illustrated* reported on the change in one quiet-spoken athlete, a professional football player. Though always tough on the field, he said that he had never wished serious harm on an opponent. But now, on being hit hard, especially with what he called "cheap shots," he really went after the opponent with every intention of hurting him in ways he had never dared before.

This new hostility was not limited to opponents. The player's wife noted that he just as quickly became hostile off the field, that he talked louder and more angrily than before, and that he had become very rough in their love-making.

There is also some recent evidence to suggest that the steroids have the power to do more than generate rough behavior. As indicated by the results of a study published in a 1988 issue of the *American Journal of Psychiatry*, they may also trigger psychotic behavior or "steroid psychosis."[5] The study was conducted by Harrison G. Pope, Jr., a psychiatrist at Harvard University's McLean Hospital in Massachusetts, and his associate, David L. Katz. The two researchers studied and interviewed forty-one heavy steroid users on both the East and West coasts. They found that 12 percent of the athletes had suffered psychotic symptoms while taking steroids. Here are two examples of what the researchers learned.

One bodybuilder burglarized six homes in his Maryland neighborhood and set fire to three of them. When apprehended by police, he was dazed and unable to give any reasons for his actions. The study found that he had never been in trouble with the law until 1985. It was then that he began taking steroids as part of his training program.

Another athlete told of his experience when he was cut off by a car while driving in traffic. He jumped to the pavement and began battering the windshield of the other car with a crowbar.

It is possible, however, that the steroids were not solely— or at all—responsible for the reported psychotic behaviors because 32 percent of the athletes interviewed also admitted to prior abuse of cocaine or marijuana. The two researchers concluded that steroids may indeed bring on psychotic behaviors, but said that the amount of the dosage needed to trigger such behaviors may prove difficult to ascertain.

It is unknown as yet whether the steroids, like such drugs as morphine and heroin, are physically addictive. But there is evidence to suggest that they may be psychologically addictive—that an athlete may so come to depend on their uplift and body-building capabilities that he or she feels unable to compete without their help.

An example of this kind of dependence is provided by one user-athlete who later became a sports official. He admits to knowing that the steroids almost killed him, but says that he couldn't give them up when he returned to competition. He felt that he could no longer win without them—even though he had been a champion performer long before ever hearing of steroids.

Athletes trying to drop the steroid habit have been known to weep openly over the problems they have faced. The close friends of one athlete are certain that he became suicidal because of the effects of the steroids and the difficulties involved with quitting.

One reason why it is difficult to drop the steroid habit has to do with a certain way that the drugs act. The steroids are effective only when they are in the system. As soon as they are stopped, much of the gain in strength and tissue growth is lost. The loss comes, no matter how hard the athlete trains to prevent it. Having won the great gains, many users can't stand the thought of losing them.

## "PLAYING WITH DYNAMITE"

The physical and psychological dangers of steroid use are showing themselves to be so awful that medical and sports authorities everywhere are loudly condemning it.

Bob Goldman, for example, told *Time* magazine that any competitor who experiments with steroids is "playing with dynamite." He added that steroid users are not just risking health problems but also death. The American College of Sports Medicine has long called for a broad program to educate athletes, coaches, trainers, physicians, and the general public on the hazards of steroid use.

In spite of these statements—and many others like them—the use of steroids to build new body tissue and enhance strength and performance has continued to grow through the years until, to repeat the words of Dr. Clayton Thomas of the U.S. Olympic Sports Medicine Council, it has reached epidemic proportions. Joining Dr. Thomas in this view is Dr. Daniel Hanley of the U.S. Olympic Committee. He says that the problem of steroid use is worse today than ever before.

When faced with so much ugly evidence, why have more and more athletes turned to the steroids? Are they blind? Stupid? Or has their need to win overcome all else and driven them to take any risk for the sake of a future victory?

The possible answers to these questions are given in our next chapter.

# 4

# ANABOLIC STEROIDS: WHY ATHLETES RISK THEM

During the early years of their history, the steroids were most often taken in ignorance. At the time, little was understood of their possible dangers. Many users simply did not realize that they were venturing into hazardous territory.

But matters are different today. The word of what the steroids can do is now widely known in the sports world. It has been spread by news reports in such magazines as *Time* and *Sports Illustrated*. It has been spread by such books as *Death in the Locker Room* by Bob Goldman, *The Sports-medicine Book* by Dr. Gabe Mirkin, *Anabolic Steroids and Sports,* volumes I and II, by Dr. James Wright, and *Drugs, Steroids and Sports* by Janet Mohun. Perhaps most effectively of all, it has been spread by athletes who are personally acquainted with the steroids—by competitors who themselves have had unhappy encounters with them or have seen their user-friends suffer.

As a result, many users have abandoned the drugs. But just as many others—perhaps even more—have ignored the warnings. And still other athletes, though fully aware of Bob Goldman's caution that they are "playing with dynamite," have begun the steroid habit.

What drives today's users to risk their health and even their lives by challenging the steroid dangers? The answer has two parts. First, it involves certain personality traits found in many athletes, especially in those who desire, above all else, to be champions. Second, it has to do with a number of pressures exerted by the sports world on modern competitors.

We'll look at each part in turn.

## THE "MUST WIN" PERSONALITY

Let's say that you participate in a sport because it gives you pleasure. You like to win, yes. Who doesn't? But winning isn't everything. What really counts is that you get to join in the fun and enjoy the companionship of your fellow players. For you, a sport is just one part of life—a fun part, indeed, but still just one part.

Millions of people the world over participate in sports in this way. But they differ greatly from the truly dedicated athlete, the athlete who wants to go as far as possible in his or her sport, who yearns to take bigger and bigger championships, and who dreams of perhaps turning professional one day. Most—if indeed not all—truly dedicated athletes are said by psychologists to have compulsive personalities. Success in their sport means *everything* to them. They feel compelled to win. Many see themselves as failed human beings if they lose.

It is this compulsiveness that drives the truly dedicated to train long hours, endure tiredness and hunger, and give up much time that could be spent relaxing with friends. They make these sacrifices because they love what they are doing, they want to win, and they want to be the best there is.

On the one hand, the deep-seated need to win and do your best is great. It accounts for many of the splendid achievements made in all lines of endeavor. But, on the other hand, it is a desire that can be dangerous if it is not handled sensibly—and this is what has happened to so many athletes who have tried steroids, especially those who have taken them without medical supervision. If taken without

**Some athletes get caught up by the
thrill of winning—at any cost.**

medical supervision, the steroids must of course be obtained illegally, from what is called the "illicit market"—from some fellow athletes, drug dealers, and unwise or unscrupulous coaches, trainers, and pharmacists. In 1986 federal authorities estimated that the illicit trade in steroids brings in $100 million annually. Three years later, *World Press Review* reported that the amount of money involved in the illegal steroid trade on the U.S. West Coast is said to be greater than that from cocaine and its derivative, crack.[1]

The overwhelming need to win and do one's best has driven some athletes to risk any danger just to get that winning edge. One ambitious weight lifter recalls a terrible experience. "I saw one of my friends collapse on the platform during a meet. His left quadricep had given out. We were both on steroids and I knew the same thing could happen to me. But I never considered stopping them. I just had to take my chances."

The same compulsion has driven some athletes to the steroids because their competitors were on them. Speaking to this point, another weight lifter remembers, "When I heard that a major opponent in my weight class had started steroids, I could think of just one thing. He's getting a big advantage. He's going to win. I couldn't let him get away with it."

And the compulsion has driven some individuals to increase their steroid consumption and thus worsen their problems. Today, a former college football star shakes his head at what he calls his "total dumbness" as he says, "I saw the great body gains that came with just a few tablets. And so I told myself, hey man, if a couple of tablets will do this much good, then twice as many will do twice as much good." It is this attitude that "more is better" that has led some athletes to consume the drug in astonishing quantities. You'll recall from Chapter Three that some doctors believe that many athletes consume from 10 to 100 times the normal steroid dosages, while other physicians think that those overdosages run from 100 to 1,000 times greater than normal.

Just how deep this compulsiveness can run in the athletic personality is exemplified in a story told by Dr. Gabe

Mirkin, the author of *The Sportsmedicine Book*. Dr. Mirkin, himself an excellent runner, recalls the time he asked 100 runners if they would take a drug that would make them Olympic champions but kill them in a year.

More than half the runners shocked him with their answer. It was yes.

In *Death in the Locker Room,* Bob Goldman writes that he was as shocked as Dr. Mirkin by that answer. He wondered if it really represented the feeling of a wide body of athletes. He decided to formulate a question of his own for 198 of his friends, most of whom were weight lifters. He asked them if they would take a drug that would enable them to win every championship meet for the next five years, even if they knew it would kill them at the end of that time.

Goldman reported that 103—or 52 percent—of the athletes expressed a willingness to take the drug. He said they understood that its use would amount to cheating because of the unfair advantage it gave. Still, they were willing to take the drug and willing to give their lives for the thrill of winning.

## THE ATHLETIC MIND-SET

In addition to a compulsive personality, many hard-driving competitors develop what is called the "athletic mind-set."

The term springs from the fact that athletes train hard for a single goal or a series of goals. Perhaps the single goal is an Olympic gold medal. Perhaps the series of goals adds up to a string of victories that carry the individual from local to national and then international competitions—or to the ranks of the professionals. Soon, it's all too easy for the athletes to think of nothing else. Put yourself in their place and you might imagine yourself saying, "I must get to where I'm going—at *any cost.*"

The case of a young woman bodybuilder in the Midwest serves as a fine illustration of what can happen here. She believed in the traditional approach to winning championships—the developing of skills, stamina, and strength through rigorous training, proper diet, and sufficient sleep.

But her friends told her that she was falling behind because her competitors were all on steroids. What chance, they asked, did she have of reaching her goal—a national championship—when her competition was getting the edge with chemical help. *She had to catch up.* At first, she shook her head adamantly. But soon the pressure and the desire to achieve her goal proved too much. She tried her first steroids.

She regrets her decision to this day, saying that the harm far outweighed the benefits.

At times, the pressure to try steroids does not come from the athletes themselves or their fellow competitors. In 1988, in the wake of the Ben Johnson scandal, Dr. Roy Bergman of the Olympic Sports Medicine Council told reporters that pressure has also been exerted by the parents of some high-schoolers. He said that a physician will often be approached by parents who ask that he or she write a steroid prescription for their son. They will explain that their son is a talented athlete but physically "a little on the small side." They feel that if the youngster were just a bit bigger he could possibly win a scholarship to play college football. Dr. Bergman said that these parents talk a great deal about the financial advantages to be gained for their son.[2]

## PRESSURES FROM THE SPORTS WORLD

While much pressure is exerted by fellow competitors and even parents, the greatest amount comes from the sports world itself, especially for those athletes who are questing after significant championships or a place in the professional ranks.

People have always loved sports. It's a love that can be traced back to ancient times—back to the Egyptians who enjoyed a form of bowling some 7,000 years ago, back to the Greeks who crowded in to see the first Olympic Games about 3,400 years ago, and back to the Chinese who played a soccerlike game 2,500 or so years ago. But, though it has always been there and though it has always been great, the love of sports is especially keen and widespread in our day. People everywhere are fascinated by athletics.

Our modern means of communication are greatly—if not mainly—responsible for this fascination. Daily, the press, television, and radio inform us of what's going on throughout the athletic world and, in so doing, have often made us fans of sports that we previously knew nothing about. They report immediately on the outcome of games and meets held anywhere on earth. Better yet, radio and television allow us to follow the meets and games as they take place. Just how many spectators can "attend" a sporting event and share in its thrills without leaving home was clearly seen in the 1984 Summer Olympics at Los Angeles, California. Loving every minute of the action, more than 2,500 million people across the world watched the Games unfold on television.

But the Olympics are not the only athletic attractions that draw huge audiences. In the United States alone, several million people annually attend or tune in to college basketball and football games. And millions more are avid followers of professional sports—football, baseball, basketball, hockey, tennis, and golf, to name a few. Even high school events that once pulled in perhaps several hundred spectators are now watched by several thousand in those cities where the competitions are telecast by local stations.

All this attention has made superheroes of athletes—especially the very top competitors. Their names are known to millions. As professionals, they command salaries that can stagger the imagination. Every fan has read of outstanding amateurs who sign professional contracts worth millions of dollars. It's common knowledge that even the average salaries in the pro football, baseball, and basketball leagues are on a par with—and often exceed—those paid to top business executives. And every sports fan knows that top performers from both the amateur and professional ranks

**The drive to win may be fed by seeing the many rewards—new careers, high salaries, public acclaim, and more— open to superstar athletes like Joe Montana.**

have the chance to win jobs that place them in the public eye. The list of successes here is long: Johnny Bench, Pat Haden, Merlin Olson, Terry Bradshaw, and John Madden have gone from the playing field to the sports announcer's booth; Joe Montana, Joe Namath, Chris Evert, and Roger Staubach have all done TV commercials; Jim Bouton, John Brodie, and Bill Walsh are just three of the many sports figures who have written best-selling books; and Alex Karras and Jim Brown have built acting careers for themselves. One of today's most firmly established facts is that success in sports can lead to a lifetime of fame and highly paid work.

And so the athletes feel a great pressure. They must always perform at their best if they hope to reach championship or professional status and the rewards to be found there. Then, on arrival, they must go on performing at their best and winning if they hope to continue reaping those rewards. As a result, many ambitious young competitors have turned to the steroids for help on the climb up the ladder. And many amateur and professional stars already at the top, growing older and nearing the end of their careers, have used the steroids in the hope of finding the strength that will enable them to remain in the limelight for as long as possible.

As if all this were not enough, there is a further pressure. It is exerted on athletes in international meets—competitors who are representing not just their team or their school, but are out there on the court or the field for their country.

## THE INTERNATIONAL PROBLEM

International meets were originally intended to promote understanding and friendship among the peoples of the world by bringing their best athletes together in amicable competitions. Through no fault of the athletes or of people in general, that intention has long been threatened. Global politics have been at fault. For years, they have intruded on the meets and have tended to make them political rather than sports events. In 1936, for example, when the Olympic Games were held in Germany, dictator Adolf Hitler planned to have his athletes post a series of triumphs that would prove the Germans to be, as he so loudly insisted, the world's "master race." Hitler's fury was reported everywhere when his plan was upset by America's splendid black track star, Jesse Owens. The dictator damaged the spirit and intent of the Games by turning his back when Owens stood proudly on the winner's stand to accept his three gold medals.

But, as bad as it was, the damage done to the 1936 Games in no way could match the damage that world politics have done to international events in the years since World War II—the years of the Cold War between the countries of the free and Communist worlds. Increasingly, political forces have turned competitions such as the Olympics into power struggles between nations—especially between the United States and the Soviet Union—rather than tests of athletic skill and prowess. The result has been to twist the purpose of the meets until, in the minds of far too many people, they have come to mean: "My country won more medals than your country, and so my country is better and stronger than yours." In effect, this situation has turned the athletes into warriors. They *must* win to prove not only their personal ability but their nation's worth.

It's a situation that makes no sense. What does an individual's ability to run, jump, or pole-vault have to do with the basic worth of his or her country? How can failure to win a medal lower that basic worth? But the situation nevertheless exists.

It irks countless fans and troubles all those athletes who share a deep camaraderie with their foreign competitors and want nothing more than pure contests of skill and prowess. In 1980 it brought us to the point where many people felt there would be no excitement in the Olympic Games that year when the United States, angry over the Soviet invasion of Afghanistan, refused to send a team to Moscow. There was the same feeling four years later when the Soviets retaliated (with the excuse that their athletes would not be adequately protected while in Los Angeles) by boycotting the 1984 Games.

Senseless though it is, the situation has put an extra pressure to win on the international competitors and has

**Political tensions can intrude on sports,
as at the 1936 Berlin Olympics, when
American black track star Jesse Owens
won three gold medals, upsetting
Adolf Hitler's plan for an athletic
and political triumph.**

been one more factor in prompting many of them to the use of steroids. The fact is that international political rivalries have long played a part in the steroid problem. They have been on the scene right from the beginning. As you'll recall from Chapter One, the drugs were initially used in the countries behind the Iron Curtain. It was the sense of international "sports warfare" that caused these countries to keep the word of the steroids secret. They wanted that winning edge all to themselves.

The rivalries were again seen as the word of the steroids fanned out across the world. As the secret of these "wonder drugs" leaked out, the coaches, trainers, and athletes of other nations were quick to try them in the hopes of snatching the winning edge away from the Communist-bloc countries. Such was the case with the first steroid use in the United States.

Steroids were introduced into the United States by the late Dr. John Ziegler, a fine physician, scientist, and athlete. Long a leading figure in United States weight lifting, Dr. Ziegler traveled to Vienna, Austria, for a 1956 championship meet. One evening while there, he went to dinner with a Russian trainer who was also a close friend. The trainer told him that the Soviet athletes had found some miracle drugs—called anabolic steroids—and were realizing tremendous strength gains from them.

Dr. Ziegler was angry that the Soviets had grabbed such an advantage. He also felt that the Russians were planning to use sports to help prove their political superiority to the world. Wanting to help his country keep up with the Soviets, the physician came home with the news of the steroids, prescribed their use for his weight-lifter friends, and worked with the CIBA Pharmaceutical Company of New Jersey to develop the first American steroid, which was marketed under the brand name Dianabol.

The doctor was always careful in his administration of the steroids. But in time he saw the compulsive athletic nature at work. Some of the competitors in his care asked for larger and larger doses. When he refused, several obtained the drug from other sources, joining a growing number of athletes who were using it on their own. And in time he saw the harm that the steroids could do and turned against them. The CIBA Company, also seeing the harm, discontinued the production of Dianabol, although the firm today manufactures other steroids.

Dr. Ziegler died in 1984. Just before his death, the man who had brought the word of the steroids home so that his nation could stay abreast of the Soviet competition said that he wished he had never heard of the drugs.

In the late 1980s, there was a lessening of the Cold War tensions between the United States and the Soviet Union because of Soviet premier Mikhail Gorbachev's *glasnost* program. There was a further lessening of tensions in 1991, following the enormous changes in the structure of the Soviet Union, and the attitudes of government leaders. Many sports figures and fans hope that the easing of tensions will have a happy effect on athletic competitions involving the two nations, and, in turn, a happy effect on the international sports scene.

By now you must be quite curious about the third point in the steroid problem—what the sports world is doing to halt its spread. But we're going to save our discussion of this point until later in the book. At that time, we'll be able to talk not only about it but also about the steps being taken to combat the use of other drugs in sports.

And what are those other drugs? Let's examine them in the next chapter.

# 5

# THE
# AMPHETAMINES

This chapter begins with the work of a Chinese emperor who lived 4,000 years ago. His name was Shen Nung. A scientist as well as a ruler, he studied and wrote about a number of plants. They possessed, in the emperor's words, "magical powers" that could relieve the suffering of the sick and injured. One was a bush he called *ma huang*.

Shen Nung described *ma huang* as a low, woody shrub with clusters of green twigs. On the twigs bloomed the tiny leaves and flowers that gave the plant its "magic." If a man stirred them into a tea, Shen Nung wrote, he would concoct a potion that could lower a fever, improve his circulation, and give him a feeling of well-being.

Today, we know *ma huang* to be the ephedra plant, which grows mainly in desert regions. And we know that its active agent—the substance responsible for those "magical powers"—is the alkaloid, ephedrine. Ephedrine is defined as a vasopressor, meaning that it stimulates the heart and circulation. Out of it have come a number of drugs that, because of these stimulating effects, are widely used in the treatment of low blood pressure, shock, and Addisonian anemia. A variety of mild ephedrine drugs, when

The ephedra plant that grows throughout
the deserts of the southwest was the original
source of the alkaloid drug, ephedrine.

inhaled, have proved of value in the relief of hay fever, asthma, and nasal congestion.

Scientist invented a synthetic form of ephedrine in the late nineteenth century. It emerged as a drug that, like Shen Nung's *ma huang*, provides a strong sense of well-being and fires the body with energy. They christened it amphetamine. The term comes from the structural name of the chemical *alpha-methyl-ph*enethyl plus *amine* (*amine* means a type of organic compound).

In the years since its invention, amphetamine has been developed into some thirty different drugs, with their differences depending on the chemical mixtures involved. They have been manufactured as tablets, capsules, inhalants, and liquids.

## THE ENERGY
## GIVERS

The amphetamines are classed as stimulant drugs because they instill that same sense of well-being—of uplift—that Shen Nung noted in *ma huang*. But it would be an understatement to say that they just make a person feel good. They do far more. They lower one's sensitivity to pain, erase the need for sleep, and fill the user with a bounding energy. This energy has earned them such familiar nicknames as uppers, wire, and pep pills. They also have nicknames that arose from the shapes of the various pills, their colors, their contents, and the rates of their action—footballs, greenies, black beauties, dexies and bennies (for the brand names, Dexedrine and Benzedrine), and speed (for the quick-acting methamphetamine). Users of speed have traditionally been known as "speed freaks."

Though their history dates back to the late nineteenth century, the amphetamines were not introduced into medical practice until the 1930s. Since then, they have helped the ill in a number of ways. For instance, they have long served in the treatment of *narcolepsy*, a rare disease that triggers the overwhelming need to sleep. They have also been used to enliven patients whose physical or emotional illnesses are causing a serious loss of energy. And, because

61

they curb one's hunger while imparting feelings of energy, the amphetamines were once widely prescribed for weight loss in cases of obesity. But they are now rarely employed in such cases.

For some odd reason that medical science has yet to understand, one amphetamine drug, methylphenidate, acts in reverse when given to hyperactive children. Rather than energizing the youngsters, it calms them. And so the drug plays a role in the treatment of children's *hyperkinesis*, a brain disorder marked by constant activity and the inability to concentrate.

Their energizing abilities have seen the amphetamines widely employed in preventive medicine over the years. They have been prescribed mainly to help safeguard individuals who must remain awake and perform well if they are to have a good chance of getting through times of exhausting physical and mental strain. Ever since World War II, many nations have distributed amphetamines to military personnel in battle. The astronauts of the troubled *Apollo 13* moon shot in 1970 took amphetamines to keep them alert throughout the long return to Earth after an oxygen tank ruptured on the outside of their spacecraft.

For some years after being introduced into medicine, the amphetamines could be obtained without a doctor's prescription. Easily obtained over the counter at drugstores, they were eagerly sought out by anyone needing extra energy. Truck drivers bought them to stay awake on long hauls. So did students who had to study through the night for a morning exam. And so did actors, musicians, and factory workers faced with a tiring night's work. But in the years following World War II, the potency of the amphetamines began to be recognized and the government declared that they could be secured only with a doctor's prescription. However, their use was not placed under the strictest of controls and they remained readily available. By 1970 the government had come to regard the amphetamines as truly dangerous drugs. As part of an overall revision of United States drug laws, Congress adopted strict regulations surrounding their administration.

## THE AMPHETAMINES AT WORK

The amphetamines work by releasing two chemicals—epinephrine and norepinephrine—from the adrenal glands and the nervous system. On release, these chemicals cause the muscles to tense, the heart to beat faster, and the blood pressure to rise. The result: the user feels energized, wide awake, and capable of much activity. Depending on the dosage taken, the period of energy and wakefulness can run from several hours to two or three days. It is, of course, followed by an extreme tiredness and the need to sleep.

When taken in small amounts or just occasionally, the amphetamines are not considered especially dangerous. Their dangers come with heavy and continued use—the sort of use that occurs when the drugs are not administered under careful medical supervision.

Heavy and continued use of amphetamines is especially dangerous because the body quickly builds a tolerance to the drugs. It requires them in increasing doses to reach the same energy highs previously achieved with lesser amounts. The amphetamines, however, are not categorized as physically addictive substances. This is because stopping their use does not bring on the painful withdrawal symptoms associated with other drugs—for example, the sweating, the runny eyes and nose, and the contorted intestines that occur with heroin withdrawal. But there is no doubt that the amphetamines are psychologically addictive, with the user often coming to think that he or she cannot function successfully without their help.

## ENERGY OUT OF CONTROL

What happens with heavy and continued use? In a nutshell, the amphetamine energy gets out of control. Users start to behave in various odd ways. Imagine for a moment that you are an amphetamine user, and consider what you will experience. You'll likely find that you simply cannot remain still, but must be up and pacing here and there. You'll also probably be hit with the overwhelming urge to talk—and talk and talk. In time you may become the victim of a condition that drives you to repeat pointless tasks or actions over and over again. You may, for instance, find yourself walking in endless circles just to be doing something. Or you may string beads for hours without knowing what you're doing, turn the pages of a book without seeing them, or write the same word a thousand or more times.

And, in time, you're more than likely to find that all the unleashed energy did not allow you to do what you set out to do. You may have wanted the energy for writing a term paper that you let go until the night before it was due. Throughout the night, you write away and think that you're doing a brilliant job. Then, on coming down from your high, you're shocked to see that what you've written is all gibberish.

Or, if you're a truck driver, you may think that you're in top form, in full control, as you roar through the darkness—only to wake up hours later in a hospital and find that you were tragically mistaken. Studies show that drivers who are heavy users suffer more accidents than nonusers, often because of their erratic behavior, often because they suddenly fall asleep when the effects of the drug wear off.

Or, if you're a football player, you may behave as a defensive lineman did one afternoon. He infuriated his coaches when, on every play, he charged to the exact same spot in the enemy backfield. The opposing team quickly took advantage of his strange habit and aimed all plays away from that spot. Time and again, the man was ordered to change his tactics. But he was powerless to obey and went on blindly repeating himself. At last, he had to be pulled out of the game.

Or, if you're a baseball player, you might suffer the experience of the big league pitcher whom Jim Bouton mentions in his book, *Ball Four*. The man felt that he was having a great day on the mound. He was sure that he had never pitched better. In fact, he was sure that he was throwing the ball as well as any big leaguer had ever thrown it. Then the manager walked out to the mound and told him that his last three pitches had been tagged for home runs.

Shaking his head in disbelief, the pitcher headed for the showers.

As a heavy and habitual user, you may well begin to hallucinate, seeing or hearing things that aren't there. The hallucinations are usually anything but pleasant. The personnel in drug treatment centers regularly hear amphetamine victims screaming that strange bugs are crawling all over them. On recovering, one such victim was astonished to learn that the "bugs" had been bits of dried skin on his arms.

No matter whether you're a heavy or a light user, you fall into a deep sleep when the drug wears off and you come down from the energy high. The letdown grows increasingly difficult for the habitual user. After the sleep, there may be the awareness of the foolish things you did, and certainly the awareness that the drug did no real good and that you're trapped in its use. These understandings can bring a deep depression and a sense of self-loathing that, in time, can become chronic. Many users, knowing the agonies that letdown can bring, take other drugs to make things easier for themselves by dulling their senses. Among the drugs most used at these times are alcohol, the barbiturates, and the treacherously addictive narcotic, heroin. The barbiturates and heroin are depressant drugs, meaning that they suppress body actions and bring on sleep.

By turning to such drugs, you begin to create an "up and down" pattern of usage that is all too familiar in the amphetamine world. Chronically depressed, you use the amphetamines to find some energy, then the depressants to help you back down, and then the amphetamines again for the next trip up.

The mental illness called *paranoia* often results from heavy and continued use. Here, your wakefulness and alertness take an odd turn. They make you suspicious of everyone around you. You begin to think that all the people you see—friends and strangers alike—are out to harm you in some way. Perhaps they want to cheat you, perhaps make fun of you, perhaps hurt you physically, perhaps even kill you. In your twisted state, you're likely to attack the suspected persons or lock yourself up at home and hide from them.

On top of all else, heavy and continued use poses the threat of death. An overdose can be—and often has been—fatal. There have been several instances of soccer and football players collapsing and dying on the field after downing too much of the drug. Further, because the amphetamines curb the appetite, some users have wasted away to the point where they no longer had the resistance to stave off or survive an illness. And any medical worker who has dealt with amphetamine use can tell you of the suicides that have resulted from the deep depression brought on by the drug.

## AMPHETAMINE ABUSE

In the years before and immediately following World War II, there was little amphetamine abuse, either by athletes or the general public. The amphetamines were used, yes, but chiefly for medical purposes. Public abuse—that is, remember, the heavy use for pleasure or an escape from life's burdens—began in the late 1950s and early 1960s, those turbulent years that saw the birth of today's worldwide drug problem. By the close of the 1960s the abuse of the amphetamines ranked right alongside that of the far more publicized drugs of the day—marijuana and LSD.

At that time, no one knew (and still no one knows) exactly how many people were abusing amphetamines. Law enforcement authorities and drug experts, however, believed that the total ran into the millions. Studies and police records showed that the users came from all walks of life and ranged from the very young (there were cases on record of preteen users) to the very old.

Some idea of how great the illegal use must have been can be gleaned from one fact. In the late 1960s some 10 billion amphetamine pills were being manufactured annually in the United States for legitimate medical purposes. At least half those pills "disappeared" each year and found their way into the illegal drug trade. They arrived there after being stolen from manufacturers' warehouses, from hospitals, from doctors' offices, drugstores, and even home medicine cabinets.

The amphetamines continue to this day to be widely abused by the public, although they've taken a backseat to another stimulant—the most popular illegal drug of the 1980s and 1990s, cocaine. Still, worldwide, the illegal amphetamine trade, fed by stolen pills and by those produced in clandestine factories (located mainly in Europe and Latin America), reaps a multi-million-dollar harvest each year. In the United States alone, the illegal sale of the amphetamines and such other drugs as the methaquaaludes (widely abused tranquilizing drugs) is estimated to be worth about $17 billion annually.

The 1950s and 1960s saw the amphetamines become as popular with athletes as with the public. This was to be expected. Competitors who had never heard of the things before now listened eagerly to the news of all the great energy to be had. Here was another way to gain that winning edge. They went for it. Since then, many of their number have suffered the harm that increasing misuse has wrought, a fact that brings us to our next chapter.

# 6

# THE AMPHETAMINES IN SPORTS

---

Though they have likely been abused by some athletes for pleasure or to escape life's problems, the amphetamines have been mostly sought after in sports as winning-edge drugs. As such, they have long been used legally. Legal use, as you know, requires a doctor's prescription.

As winning-edge drugs, the amphetamines have mainly been prescribed in those sports that call for a tremendous amount of stamina and endurance. Cyclists facing long races, for instance, have taken them. So have football, soccer, and baseball players readying themselves for an afternoon of hard action. The same goes for track-and-field competitors in need of a sudden burst of energy.

Similarly, the amphetamines have been used in sports that impose weight limits on the competitors. To mention just three examples, they have been prescribed for boxers, wrestlers, and jockeys dieting to make weight requirements.

And, as winning-edge drugs, the amphetamines have been called on to serve the needs of certain athletes at certain times. Here we're talking about players who, as reporter Barry Lorge wrote in a series of articles for the

*Washington Post,* are "going all out in the last period of any exhausting game" and competitors who are up against almost unendurable demands: "a cross-country skier or cyclist facing the last hills of a grueling journey . . . a 35-year-old football player who no longer has the spring in his legs of the 25-year-old across the line from him . . . a sprinter who has to toe the mark in a meet where fractions of a second loom unimaginably long . . . a sore-armed relief pitcher trying to get through the last days of a 162-game season . . . or a javelin thrower who knows that an Olympic medal depends on one's backlog of quality training, and needs a little extra pep to get him through the days when he doesn't feel like training."[1]

Of the sports mentioned above, football must be singled out for extra attention. Here amphetamine use seems to be especially widespread, particularly in the professional ranks. In fact, amphetamine use in professional football is widely recognized by sports authorities as being a greater and more enduring problem than in pro baseball, basketball, and hockey. There are two reasons for this. First, the game is a hard-hitting, bone-crunching test of strength (in many ways, even a harsher test than hockey). The players know that the painkilling capabilities of the amphetamines will help them to take and dish out the game's continual and jarring hits.

That the amphetamines are used to dull pain can be seen from the player positions where they are said to be most used. Studies show that linemen are more likely than backfield men to be amphetamine users. Special teams, famous for the bruising punishment that they must absorb, also have a reputation as users. For years they have been known within the National Football League as "greeny squads" (because the pills are green in color).

Second, there is the nature of the game itself. Players know that it is most successfully played when there is confidence and a sense of controlled anger. The amphetamines help to provide that confidence and controlled anger.

The amphetamines are said to be especially popular among older professional football players. In the eyes of most doctors, the reason for this popularity is obvious. As

Amphetamines' capacity to dull pain has led to its abuse among athletes who are part of the bone-crunching action on the football field.

one doctor has put it. "The older player's body has taken years of punishment and is feeling the cumulative effects. And age is catching up with him. He's not as able to absorb punishment as he was ten years ago. And he knows it. The amphetamines dull the pain and give him the feeling that, for at least a little while longer, he's as good as he ever was."

Another theory is offered by Dr. Arnold Mandell, a research psychiatrist and a former consultant to the San Diego Chargers. Mandell believes that the controlled rage is connected to certain brain chemicals whose actions decrease with advancing age. He says that it is quite easy for, say, a nineteen-year-old to "psych" himself up—gather that controlled rage—for a game. But the rage builds more slowly and reaches lower heights as the years go by. As Dr. Mandell sees it, the player in his mid-thirties is simply unable to make himself angry enough. He then turns to the amphetamines to bring on the anger that the brain chemicals once induced so easily.

## A CHANGE FROM EARLIER DAYS

But now one important point must be made. Though they can be legally prescribed, the amphetamines are not as much used today as they once were. In the 1960s, before their dangers were fully recognized and before the government's 1970 adoption of strict regulations concerning their use, uppers were freely dispensed in American locker rooms, especially those at the professional level. Just listen to some of the memories from that time:

Baseball's Johnny Bench was just breaking into the major leagues. He recalls that the team trainers always had Dexamyl and Darprisal pills (two popular brand names of amphetamines) in ample supply. In his autobiography, *Catch You Later,* he writes that no one, neither trainer nor player, was concerned about handing them out in generous quantities before game time.

Similar recollections come from professional football and basketball. Several National Football League veterans, among them tight end Jean Fugett, say that when they entered play in the late 1960s or early 1970s, amphetamine use was commonplace. It was not considered especially dangerous and was joked about by their fellow players. In a 1979 interview for the *Washington Post,* pro basketball star Paul Silas said that the taking of uppers was widespread among players when he joined the National Basketball Association (NBA) in 1964.

Silas, however, pointed out that amphetamine use in the NBA had dropped significantly since then. He said that years ago many players lived too hard off the court, staying up late to drink and play cards. Exhausted the next day, they turned to the stimulants to get "up" for a game. But now they were making astronomical salaries, and were meeting their responsibilities to those salaries by taking care of themselves. As Silas saw it, they no longer needed the help of the pills. Additionally, he mentioned the speed and mental sharpness required for pro basketball. Silas said flatly that players simply can't handle the game's lightning-fast action and constant demand for quick thinking if they're downing what he called "all kinds of stuff."

The move away from the heavy use of the 1960s began early in the 1970s. In 1970 itself, the United States replaced its earlier drug laws with the Comprehensive Drug Abuse Prevention and Control Act. The act set forth strict regulations for the production, sale, and use of all dangerous drugs—narcotics, stimulants, depressants, and hallucinogens (drugs able to make a user hallucinate). As stimulants, the amphetamines were included in the act. As had been the case during the years following World War II, they were to be available only with a doctor's prescription, but were now to be more strictly regulated than ever before in their administration. The major professional sports groups—the two baseball leagues, the National Football League, the National Basketball Association, and the National Hockey League—quickly responded to the act. Concerned over the growing drug problem in sports, they all established anti-drug policies (we'll see exactly what they did when we come to Chapter Eleven). The amphetamines were affected in two ways by the policies. The leagues began routinely checking the amounts prescribed by team physicians, a practice that has continued ever since. And team physicians and trainers were charged with taking extra care in their administering of the drugs.

## THE PROBLEM REMAINS

Despite all these steps, the amphetamine problem did not disappear. The situation remained the same, as with other winning-edge drugs. Those players who wanted more amphetamines than could be legitimately obtained turned to outside sources, including the illegal market, for their supplies. And the result? It is the same as with other drugs: an undisciplined and unsupervised misuse.

This misuse led to some sad consequences. Since an increase in a player's aggressiveness can go hand in hand with his or her rising energy, the suspicion is widespread that heavy amphetamine use is behind some exceptionally rough football action that has ended in injury. Further, a number of football and baseball players suspect that they've seen paranoid behavior during games. In the faces of some teammates and opponents, they've glimpsed expressions that go beyond the intensity that is normal in the heat of competition. As one player has put it, "Those guys looked and acted as if they hated you. You felt they were trying to get back at you for some dirt you had done them. I like hard play, but not that kind. It's downright dangerous."

These are all suspicions. They're bad enough. But there are proven cases of the harm that the amphetamines have done.

Reporter Barry Lorge, in his series on drugs for the *Washington Post,* dwelt on one especially sad case. It concerned a California track-and-field star who, as Lorge reported, "became accustomed to popping a couple of uppers before every track meet in Long Beach, where he was the leading high school shot-putter in the country" during the early 1970s. "He increased his drug intake during an ill-fated college career, and went on several legendary drug-induced rampages.

"The most notorious came after the 1976 Pacific-Eight Conference championships." The athlete, a star at the University of California at Los Angeles (UCLA), was favored to win the shot put, but "came in a disappointing second. Although fortified by a massive dose of amphetamine, he 'unwound' with tranquilizers and then, in the words of a witness, 'just went beserk.' "

Lorge wrote that the athlete, who weighed more than 300 pounds (140 kg), "practically dismantled his motel room, then tied four bed sheets together, strapped a fire extinguisher on his back, and leapt Tarzan-style off a fourth-floor balcony. . . . Instead of swinging to another balcony, however, his arc sent him crashing through a plate glass window and into a first-floor room. UCLA wound up with a $3,500 bill." The young man escaped serious injury.

The incident was bad enough in itself. But there was more to come. The athlete transferred to another school for a time and then returned to UCLA, but was dismissed after the 1977 track season. He finally enrolled at California State College–Long Beach, only to become angry with the coach there and threaten him with a beating, a threat that eventually earned him a month in jail.

Later, because he had also been an All-American defensive tackle while in high school, the Dallas Cowboys gave the young man a tryout. The club soon dropped him, however, on learning that he was awaiting trial for his trouble at Cal State.

Barry Lorge finished the athlete's story with the report: "Friends say that he is now a professional wrestler in Canada, awaiting a tryout with a Canadian Football League team."

Tragic as it was, the story at least did not end in death. The same cannot be said of two other stories. They're about two great European cyclists, Englishman Tommy Simpson and Frenchman Yves Mottin.

During a 1967 international race in France, Simpson suddenly began to weave back and forth across the road in the middle of one lap. He fought to regain control, but then lost consciousness and pitched over on his side. He died several hours later without ever coming out of his coma. When an autopsy was performed, a heavy amount of the extremely potent amphetamine drug, methamphetamine, was found in his system. A vial of the drug had also been discovered in his pocket.

As for Mottin, he collapsed and died two days after winning a major French cross-country race. Heavy amphetamine consumption was blamed for his death.

## CONTROLS AND
## A HEALTHY CHANGE
## OF DIRECTION

The growing heavy use of various drugs by athletes over the years has caused the sports world to adopt increasingly strict control measures. These measures have had an effect on the use of amphetamines. The amphetamines are now—and have been for a number of years—among the drugs that, if detected in the body during post-event urine tests, can cause an athlete to be disqualified from such competitions as the Olympics. In addition, the amphetamines have been carefully monitored and administered by the professional sports leagues in the United States since the passage of the Comprehensive Drug Abuse Prevention and Control Act in 1970.

Along with the United States, a number of other countries have adopted strict drug-control laws that affect the use of amphetamines. One such nation is France. The French laws enabled the country to put two of cyclist Mottin's friends on trial for providing him with the amphetamines that took his life.

Fortunately, there seems to be a healthy change of direction in the amphetamine picture. A number of studies and the remarks of many amateur and professional athletes indicate that usage of the drug has been on a downhill slide for a number of years. Though still alarmingly widespread, amphetamine use reached its peak in the early 1980s and then dropped steadily throughout the decade.

The factors mentioned above—from the post-event testing and the professional league monitoring to the strong government regulations—are given much of the credit for the declining use. As much, if not more, credit is given to the athletes themselves. More and more of them are taking

seriously the word of just how efficiently these energy-giving uppers can damage a career and a life.

In addition to those just mentioned, there is yet another factor. It may well be the one most responsible for causing so many athletes to toss out their pills. It is an ironic fact that has come to light in the past few years. The amphetamines, despite releasing all that energy and confidence, have been found to contribute nothing to a victory.

Tests held after recent Olympic meets showed that the losers all had amphetamines in their systems. And the winners? Very few showed any trace of the drugs.

However, it must be said in closing that the picture of amphetamine use today is not a completely happy one. *JAMA* reported in 1990 that the amphetamines, while falling out of favor elsewhere, have been gaining in popularity among some high school football players. *JAMA* reported that, during recent studies of steroid use among adolescents, researchers also heard a number of players admit to taking amphetamines before games to increase aggressiveness.[2]

The hope is that these young players will soon follow the example set by the older amateurs and professionals who have abandoned the drug.

**In 1965, bicycle racer Tommy Simpson celebrated after winning the World Professional Road Race Championship. After a 1967 race, he collapsed and died, with evidence of a heavy amphetamine dose in his system.**

# 7

# BRAKING
# AND BOOSTING

—

The anabolic steroids have found a place in sports because they help to build new body tissue. In this chapter, we're going to look first at some drugs that achieve a quite different effect. They are called brake drugs. Their name comes from their ability to retard—or "put the brakes on"—a certain type of body development.

Then we'll turn to a procedure that increases a person's stamina without the use of drugs. Instead of drugs, the athlete's own blood does the job. The process is called blood boosting.

## THE BRAKE DRUGS

Although it is not definitely known whether brake drugs are used in athletics, their use is strongly suspected. The suspicion centers on many of the female gymnasts who competed for the Communist-bloc countries. In their mid to late teens, these gymnasts were of the size and build of ten- or eleven-year-old girls.

In the book *Death in the Locker Room*, Bob Goldman mentions three of the young women, Elena Mukhina, Natalya Shaposhnikova, and Maria Filatova—superb performers who represented the Soviet Union when the 1978 Gymnastics Championships were held in France. At the time, at age eighteen, Elena stood just 5 feet (152 cm) tall and weighed 92 pounds (42 kg). Both Nataliya and Maria were seventeen. Natalya reached but 4 feet, 9 inches (145 cm) and weighed 79 pounds (36 kg). Maria was 4 feet, 5 inches (135 cm). Her weight was 65 pounds (29 kg).

What is to be gained from the suspected administration of brake drugs by team physicians and trainers? Quite simply, the drugs kept the Communist-bloc athletes small in a sport where smallness provides a winning edge. They do so by delaying the arrival of puberty, the age at which the female becomes capable of bearing children. When puberty is delayed, so are the physical changes that accompany it—among them the development of the breasts and the widening of the hips. These are changes that bring an increase in weight and a shift in the body's center of gravity, both of which adversely affect the gymnast's performance.

The drugs add to that winning edge in yet another way. The gymnasts have trained for several years as little girls. Were puberty allowed to occur, each gymnast would be placed at a disadvantage by having to accustom herself to the physical changes that it induces. The brake drugs not only permit her to compete for a time longer with a small body but also with one that is completely familiar to her.

A variety of drugs can be used for braking. Medically, they serve a number of valuable purposes, among them the treatment of certain cancers. Of the drugs that are perhaps being used in sports, two have come under particular suspicion—*medroxyprogesterone acetate* and *cyproterone acetate*. The term "acetate" means that the two contain a salt of acetic acid.

### Medroxyprogesterone Acetate

Medroxyprogesterone acetate is a synthetic drug that is derived from progesterone. Progesterone itself is an estrogen, meaning that it is a female hormone. The acetate is usually taken orally.

To understand the workings of the acetate, it is neces-

sary to see the role that progesterone plays in the two basic functions in the female reproductive cycle—ovulation and menstruation. When the female ovulates—passes an egg (the ovum) from one or the other of the ovaries to the uterus—progesterone is produced in the ovaries. The hormone prepares the lining of the uterus to hold and nourish an embryo should the egg be fertilized with a sperm from a male.

If there is no fertilization, the production of progesterone dips and the egg is freed from the woman's body through menstruation. Should the egg be fertilized, the progesterone continues to be produced at a significant level. The ovaries manufacture it for about three months, after which it is produced in the placenta, the membrane organ in which the fetus grows. The high level of progesterone keeps the mother from ovulating and menstruating again until after the child's birth. Since both ovulation and menstruation have to do with an egg that has yet to be fertilized, both are unnecessary during pregnancy.

Just as it does in the pregnant woman, a high level of progesterone suppresses ovulation and menstruation in a woman not pregnant. When they are suppressed in a girl at puberty, there is, at the same time, a suppression of the hormones that bring about the physical changes that go with womanhood. Those changes—increased breast and hip size—are needed to help prepare the female to bear offspring. But, without ovulation, there can be no offspring. So the body sees no need to advance into womanhood. The girl remains—as do the gymnasts thought to be receiving medroxyprogesterone acetate—a child in build and size.

**In the 1970s, the childlike appearance of a number of Soviet gymnasts, including Natalya Shaposhnikova, age 14, raised questions about the possible use of brake drugs.**

In fairness, it must be stressed again that it is still only suspected that the Communist-bloc countries used brake drugs—but it is a suspicion that makes a great deal of sense. As a number of sports physicians have pointed out, the presence on the same teams of so many teenage athletes with the petite bodies of little girls gives rise to thought. Can it all be mere coincidence? It hardly seems likely. On the other hand, it is quite possible that the rigorous diet and hours of hard training demanded in the Communist-bloc countries could account, perhaps totally or in very great part, for the petiteness.

A strict diet was certainly used by the Romanian women's gymnastics team, whose splendid Nadia Comaneci was a major star at the 1976 Olympics. In 1977, Comaneci and her teammates toured the United States. During the journey of two weeks, they ate just five meals, which consisted mainly of tomatoes and lettuce supplemented by vitamin pills.

The aim of the team's strict diet and rigorous training schedule was to keep a gymnast's fat content at less than 3 percent of her weight. This, the Romanian coaches feel, will postpone puberty and the unwelcome body changes that accompany it.

The Communist-bloc countries denied that their women gymnasts were given brake drugs.

### Cyproterone Acetate

Cyproterone acetate is a synthetic drug that is available in Europe but not worldwide. It is classed as an antihormonal substance. This means that it is able to curb the actions of various hormones.

One of the hormones against which it acts with particular success is testosterone, the male hormone at the base of many of the steroids. Since testosterone provides the male's sex drive, cyproterone acetate is widely prescribed in Europe to control the behavior of hypersexed (overly sexed) males. It is often ordered by the courts for men who have committed sex crimes such as rape, child molestation, and indecent exposure.

Sports doctors believe that cyproterone can be used as

a brake drug for women because it is not just an antitestosterone agent but a general antihormonal drug as well. In women it would block the action of the hormones responsible for their sexual growth.

### Birth Control Pills
Though they are not actually brake drugs, birth control pills must be mentioned here because of their effect on the woman competitor's reproductive cycle. Many women athletes use them, but not for birth control purposes. Rather, they take the pills to adjust their reproductive cycles so that they will not menstruate during times of competition.

## BLOOD
## BOOSTING

Blood boosting, as was earlier mentioned, is a procedure that can be used for providing increased stamina. Also known in sports as blood packing and blood doping, it is based on the fact that our red blood cells carry the oxygen that provides us with energy and endurance.

The procedure stems from the work of a Swedish scientist, Dr. Bjorn Ekblom of the Stockholm Institute of Gymnastics and Sports. In a 1972 experiment on increased energy, Dr. Ekblom removed approximately a quart of blood from each of four subjects. He then separated the red cells from the blood and placed them under refrigeration. The subjects were given four weeks in which to replenish the lost blood. At the end of that time, Dr. Ekblom reintroduced the red cells into each subject. They joined the red cells in the replenished blood supply.

The result: The four subjects, each with an excess of red cells, had the energy to run longer on a treadmill before becoming exhausted. They displayed an increase of 25 percent in endurance.

A simple theory lay behind the Ekblom experiment. The muscles require oxygen to perform. The oxygen is carried in the red cells. The more red blood cells there are, the more oxygen there will be. Hence, longer performances can be had by adding to—or boosting—the number of red cells. Technically, this approach is called *induced erythro-cythemia*—the introduction of surplus red blood cells.

Dr. Ekblom carried out his experiment in the name of pure research. He did not intend that his procedure be actually used in competition. But because of the winning edge it promises, blood boosting has been tried in several sports throughout the years since 1972. It is said to work best in events that demand stamina for extended periods of time and that call for the prolonged repetition of the same muscle movements. Among the athletes who have experimented with the procedure are Nordic cross-country skiers in Europe, racing cyclists in both Europe and the United States, and weight trainers going after a record number of repeated actions at an increased speed. Boosting is not considered useful in events requiring short bursts of energy.

## MATTERS OF
## ETHICS AND HEALTH

The ethics of blood boosting and the possible health problems it poses have long been debated in the sports world. There is divided opinion on both matters.

From an ethical standpoint, blood boosting is widely regarded as unfair because of the strong edge it can give a competitor. On the other hand, the argument has often been heard in the United States that the boosting is necessary to bring our athletes up to par with Russian and other Eastern-bloc competitors, who are strongly suspected of employing the procedure. (Once more, the rivalries that have for so long characterized international meets such as the Olympic Games can be seen).

In matters of health, many doctors find boosting hazardous. They argue that the danger of infection looms from the needles and other sources when the blood cells are being reintroduced into the athlete's system, especially when the infusion is not being carried out under medical supervision. Another of their greatest fears is that the muscles, performing beyond the time when exhaustion would be normally felt, will damage a heart that has been forced to pump too hard.

Other doctors feel that the procedure is reasonably safe when administered under medical supervision. For substantiation, they point to research that has been done at York University in Toronto, Canada. As reported in a 1985 issue of *Sports Illustrated,* the results of the research have tended to remove the fear that the heart will pump too hard to keep up with the constantly working muscles. The research found that, along with the other muscles, the myocardium (the muscle of the heart) receives an extra supply of oxygen. That extra supply helps the heart to cope with the excess strain.

There is one point, though, on which all sports physicians agree. They say that a *second* type of blood boosting is far more dangerous and should be avoided. In this procedure the athletes receive not their own blood but that of a friend or relative. Such transfusions pose the threat of needle infection (especially, again, if there is no medical supervision), plus the possibility that a perfectly healthy athlete will be infected with an illness carried by the blood donor—perhaps hepatitis, mononucleosis, or even AIDS (acquired immune deficiency syndrome).

## A NEW
## BOOSTER

The late 1980s brought a new development to the boosting scene, one that modifies our definition of blood boosting as a drug-free procedure. The new development has nothing to do with reintroducing, or transfusing, red blood cells into an athlete's system. Rather, it resulted from the appearance on the market of a new, medically useful drug. When injected into the body, the drug increases the production of the oxygen-carrying red cells. Its name is erythropoetin. It has quickly come to be called simply EPO.[1]

EPO was developed to serve a variety of medical purposes and has since served them well. It can, for instance, benefit cancer patients whose blood is weakened by chemotherapy treatments. When given to patients suffering kidney disease, it can help to repair blood that has been damaged by kidney dialysis. And it can counter the anemia that is brought on by a major drug used in the treatment of AIDS.

As medically valuable as it is proving to be, EPO is becoming a drug of concern to sports figures and sports medicine authorities. They fear that a growing number of athletes—on learning that it increases the production of the oxygen-carrying red blood cells and, as a result, brings an increase in energy—will turn to it as a winning-edge drug.

There is some strong evidence that EPO enhances athletic performance to a significant degree. In 1989 seven athletes underwent EPO testing. After being injected with the drug, they all outperformed themselves. One of the test subjects, cross-country skier Lars Erik Palmgren, reported that he was able to work on a treadmill for a longer period of time and a steeper angle than ever before.

Dr. Bjorn Ekblom assisted in the giving of the test. On seeing the results, he noted that the drug's ability to increase oxygen levels in the blood may end up cutting as many as thirty seconds off a twenty-minute running time. If so, this would make a major difference in the outcome of world-class running events, where fractions of a second usually separate the winners from the losers.

EPO can be given safely under strict medical supervision, but a number of doctors and sports authorities fear that it may raise havoc among athletes who have the "more is better" mentality. If they take the drug without the assistance of a physician and keep increasing the dosage, as so many have done with the anabolic steroids, they may run the risk of severe, even fatal, harm. Even though the research at Toronto's York University indicates that "normal" boosting (the kind involving blood transfers) will not damage the heart, there is the fear that excessive doses of a drug may well put the athletes in danger of high blood pressure, blood clots, strokes, and heart attacks.

The drug was approved in June 1989 by the federal Food and Drug Administration for medical use and may be obtained in the United States only with a doctor's prescription. A month later, the National Collegiate Athletic Association banned its use by college competitors.

# 8

# COCAINE:
# THE DRUG OF
# THE 1980s AND 1990s

It's time now to turn from the misuse of the medical drugs to the abuse of the so-called recreational drugs. In this chapter and the next, we'll be talking about cocaine and the damage it is doing in sports today. Then we'll devote a chapter to another of today's most abused recreational drugs, marijuana.

The lion's share of our attention will be concentrated on cocaine rather than marijuana. There are three reasons for this.

First, the current abuse of cocaine, by both athletes and the general public, is known to be especially widespread. In fact, the abuse has been so widespread that cocaine was christened the drug of the 1980s and is now being called the drug of the 1990s.

Second, cocaine is being employed in sports in a way that marijuana is not. Though still classified as a recreational drug, cocaine is no longer being sought by athletes just for the passing pleasure or escape from life's trials that it can provide. Many competitors are treating cocaine as if it were a medical drug. They are gambling that the energy it induces will give them that winning edge.

Finally, more than marijuana, it has written a particularly sad page in the sports history of the 1980s and now the 1990s. It has either damaged or ruined several dozen fine careers in that time. They have been the careers of not only some of the world's best but also *best-known* athletes.

## A SLOW CLIMB
## TO POPULARITY

The Inca Indians of ancient Peru, as you'll recall from Chapter One, stirred the leaves of their coca plant in hot ashes and then held the mixture in their mouths when it cooled. The mixture deadened their tongues and—a miracle so far as the Indians were concerned—filled their bodies with great energy and erased the need to sleep. The Incas used the magical concoction for needed extra energy in sporting contests and especially when heading out on long hunts or into battle.

Responsible for the energy, of course, was cocaine. Classified today as a stimulant drug and known worldwide simply as "coke," it is now understood to be so potent and dangerous that its production and traffic (except for a few medical purposes) are outlawed in a number of countries, the United States among them. It is a violation of United States federal law to cultivate, process, sell, or even possess cocaine. Conviction on any of these counts can bring stiff sentences—for instance, from several months to several years for possession, and from one to fifteen years for selling. The state laws against cocaine vary across the country. But they, too, can range from a few months in prison on a minor count of possession to years for a serious selling offense.

Long known only in South America, cocaine made its way, as we'll see later, to Europe and the United States in the late nineteenth century. It was not widely used in these areas for many years. In fact, it was such a stranger in the United States that it was rarely mentioned when today's drug abuse problem first took shape in the late 1950s and early 1960s. At that time, the nation's drug treatment centers saw but a handful of cocaine victims. The era's principal drugs of abuse were LSD, marijuana, heroin, and the amphetamines.

This situation changed, however, in the early 1970s. For reasons still not clearly understood, cocaine caught on with segments of the American population and began to win an increasing popularity. Its popularity grew steadily until cocaine, instilling its feelings of great energy and confidence, became the principal drug of abuse of the 1980s. At mid-decade, the federal government estimated that between 15 and 20 million Americans had tried cocaine.

Among the Americans who have turned to the drug have been some of the nation's top sports stars. Virtually all of them are to be found in the professional ranks. Why? Because, though its price varies from time to time and from place to place, cocaine is an expensive drug. In the United States today, it generally sells for between $70 and $100 a gram.[1] (At one time—in the early to mid-1980s—it was bringing in as much as $100 to $150 a gram. We'll talk later in the chapter about why the price has dropped in recent years.)

But just who in the professional ranks have had their careers and reputations damaged by cocaine over the past years? This question perhaps can be best answered by looking at one or two sports at a time. Let's begin with our national pastime, baseball.

## COCAINE IN BASEBALL

In 1984 *Sports Illustrated* listed the names of sixteen major league players who had been convicted or treated for the abuse of hard drugs—cocaine, marijuana, alcohol, or some combination of the three—during the preceding five-year period. Included among them were the following:

**1982** □ Outfielder Alan Wiggins of the San Diego Padres is arrested for the possession of cocaine. The charges against him are dropped when he completes the drug rehabilitation program at a CareUnit hospital in southern California. CareUnit hospitals are a group of drug and alcohol rehabilitation centers. Bowie Kuhn, the commissioner of baseball at the

time, suspends Wiggins from play for thirty days, after which Wiggins returns to the Padres and then plays a major role in the team's 1984 championship season. (Alan Wiggins died in January 1991 at age thirty-two. Pneumonia, tuberculosis, and other medical complications were given as the cause of his death.)[2]

**1982–1983** ☐ During the 1982 season, Los Angeles Dodgers relief pitching ace Steve Howe is treated at the Meadows, an Arizona rehabilitation center, for cocaine and alcohol abuse. Howe begins the 1983 season with fine appearances on the mound, but then checks into CareUnit for further treatment. While there, he is out of action for thirty days. Commissioner Kuhn, impatient with Howe's continuing abuse, fines him $53,867—an amount equal to the pitcher's salary for that thirty-day period.

**1983–1984** ☐ First baseman Willie Aikens of the Kansas City Royals and teammates, outfielders Jerry Martin and Willie Wilson, are convicted of attempting to buy cocaine. Sentenced at the same time is former Royals pitcher Vida Blue. They all serve eighty-one–day sentences at the Fort Worth Correctional Facility. Blue goes on to CareUnit for rehabilitation treatment. The four are suspended from play for a time by Commissioner Kuhn.

**1984** ☐ Atlanta Braves pitcher Pascual Perez is convicted in his homeland, the Dominican Republic, on charges of possessing cocaine. He is suspended from professional ball in the United States for several months.

**Alan Wiggins was one of the major league baseball players who was treated for drug abuse. He died in 1991, at the age of thirty-two.**

The next years brought further scandals. For example:

**1985**  ☐  At the end of a fourteen-day trial, a Pittsburgh jury convicts Curtis Strong, a caterer and former clubhouse cook, on charges of selling cocaine to major-league players between 1980 and 1983. Specifically, Strong is convicted of selling the drug on eleven dates to four players. At the time of the trial, three of the players are with the Los Angeles Dodgers, the Cincinnati Reds, and the Kansas City Royals. The fourth is a former outfielder with the Pittsburgh Pirates. They all had been with different teams when the sales were made. During the trial, Strong is called "a traveling salesman of cocaine" by the prosecution.

**1987**  ☐  Pitcher Dwight Gooden is suspended from play with the New York Mets for cocaine use and misses the first six weeks of the season. He undergoes rehabilitation for a month at the Smithers Center in Manhattan and returns to the team. In 1990 reporter Joseph Durso of the *New York Times* writes that Gooden now seems older and wiser because of two successes—his efforts to overcome drugs, and to heal the torn muscle in his right shoulder that cut short his 1989 season. The 100-game winner tells Durso that he is putting the 1980s behind him and is looking forward to pitching throughout the 1990s.[3]

**1987–1988**  ☐  The new commissioner of baseball, Peter Ueberroth, suspends pitcher Hoyt Lamar of the San Diego Padres for one year on charges of cocaine use. Lamar serves a forty-five–day sentence following his release from the Padres. In 1988 the Chicago White Sox invite him to try out for the team, but he is arrested when law enforcement officials find a cache of cocaine and marijuana in his apartment.[4]

**After completing treatment for cocaine abuse, New York Mets pitcher Dwight Gooden returned to the pitching mound.**

## COCAINE IN FOOTBALL

The cocaine problem, of course, isn't limited to baseball. It has also permeated the ranks of professional football. In 1983 the Miami Dolphins' great running back, Eugene "Mercury" Morris, was sentenced to twenty years on charges of cocaine dealing.

That same year saw four other players in the headlines for possessing cocaine. They were defensive back Greg Stemrick of the New Orleans Saints, linebacker E. J. Junior of the St. Louis Cardinals, and fullback Pete Johnson and defenseman Ross Browner, both of the Cincinnati Bengals. All were brought to court on felony charges of possessing cocaine. Stemrick and Junior were found guilty and given a year's sentence. Johnson and Browner won immunity from conviction by telling the court that they had made more than a dozen cocaine purchases from a dealer. Browner said that he had made from twelve to fifteen buys. Johnson admitted to approximately fifteen purchases.

National Football League commissioner Pete Rozelle (who served until 1989, when he retired and was replaced by NFL attorney Paul Tagliabue) suspended the quartet for four games in the 1983 season. The suspensions meant a loss in pay of $25,850 for Stemrick, $33,350 for Junior, $34,600 for Johnson, and $37,600 for Browner.

In August 1983, Tony Peters of the Washington Redskins was one of seven people charged with conspiring to distribute cocaine. The defensive back entered a plea of guilty and was sentenced to two concurrent four-year prison terms. The sentences were suspended, however, and Peters was fined $10,000, placed on probation, and ordered to perform 500 hours of community service. At the same time, he was suspended from NFL play. The suspension was lifted in the summer of 1984 because of his excellent conduct and community service while on probation.

Two of the greatest drug tragedies in professional football occurred in 1986 and 1988.[5] In 1986 Don Rogers, a defensive back with the Cleveland Browns, died in what physicians later confirmed to be a cocaine-related death. Two years later, on October 10, 1988, cornerback David

**Don Rogers, a football player with the Cleveland Browns, died in a cocaine-related death in 1986.**

Croudip suffered a seizure and heart failure a few hours after his Atlanta Falcons had been defeated 33–0 by the Los Angeles Rams. Medical authorities announced that cocaine was the probable cause of death, explaining that the drug had been found in samples of blood and urine taken from his body.

Croudip's wife told doctors that sometime during the hours following the game her husband had prepared and downed a drink in which cocaine was mixed with water or fruit juice. Depression over personal and career problems (for one, he had been worrying that he had not been playing well for the Falcons) and the loss to the Rams were thought to be the reasons the twenty-nine-year-old player had stirred up the cocaine "cocktail."

Team officials and Croudip's friends and family were shocked by the death and the word that it was due to cocaine overdose. Rankin M. Smith, the president of the Falcons, said that Croudip had never tested positive in any of the drug checks required by the National Football League. The player's friends and family said that they could not believe that he used drugs of any type because he was always deeply interested in keeping his body in the best condition possible.

## COCAINE IN BASKETBALL AND SOCCER

Basketball seems to have suffered less drug abuse than either baseball or football. In 1979 the *Washington Post* interviewed several National Basketball Association players and found that they did not regard cocaine abuse as a major problem. They said that the abusers kept their habits away from the basketball court, did not allow cocaine to interfere with the quality of their play, and were always clear-minded and ready to perform at the opening buzzer. One player remarked that not many NBA cagers were "into coke."

These, of course, were the opinions of just a few players who might have been protecting the reputations of their league, their fellow players, and themselves. But one fact indicates that they might well have been painting an accurate picture. As of the time this book is being written, basketball has been hit with but a few drug cases.

One involved Marvin Barnes, who played back in the 1970s with the now defunct American Basketball Association and then with the NBA; in his five years in pro ball, he spent time with Buffalo, St. Louis, and Detroit. He was jailed on cocaine charges for a time and was released in October 1990. Reporter Bill Reynolds of the *Providence Journal* (Rhode Island) interviewed Barnes the following month and wrote that the former player had used his time in jail wisely. Realizing that he was running out of chances to lead a productive life, he had broken his drug habit and had finished his degree work at Providence College. Barnes, the reported added, had later obtained a job in public relations and wanted to devote much of his time to warning young people of the dangers of drug abuse.[6]

The saddest instance of drug abuse in basketball comes not from the professional but the amateur ranks. In 1986 twenty-two-year-old Len Bias, a star with the University of Maryland team and a top candidate for entry into the NBA, died of what was described as "cocaine intoxication." Bias was the first of three well-known athletes to lose his life because of cocaine within a two-year period. The others were the previously mentioned Don Rogers, who died just eight days after Bias, and David Croudip.[7]

## TWO POINTS TO REMEMBER

Two points must always be remembered about the above cases. First, while they are all tragic, with some interrupting careers, some destroying careers, and some ending in death, it must be stressed that many seem to have ended on a positive note. For instance, the conduct of defensive back Tony Peters while on probation certainly gave strong indication that he was putting his problem behind him. Outfielder Willie Aiken, when he returned to play with a new team, the Toronto Blue Jays, told reporters that his time in jail did him good by keeping him away from drugs and alcohol. Marvin Barnes used his time in jail to prepare for a new life by breaking his drug habit and completing his

college degree. And remember what Dwight Gooden told reporter Joseph Durso—that he was rid of his troubles of the 1980s and was looking forward to pitching throughout the '90s.

Second, the cases must not lead to the impression that *every* professional and collegiate athlete abuses cocaine (or any other drug for that matter). Nor must there be the impression that *most* do. Both are mistaken and unfair ideas. For example, easily more than 12,000 professionals have played baseball and football during the cocaine era; they have come from varied backgrounds and have brought with them diverse viewpoints on health and morality, and so it is impossible to think that they have all decided in favor of drug abuse—or that even the majority of them have done so. There are just too many different kinds of personalities involved for that sort of thing to happen.

But then how widespread, really, is the cocaine problem? On the basis of data collected over the years, the extent of the abuse of cocaine and other drugs seems to be small in the professional ranks. In one five-year period, for instance, only sixteen baseball players out of the several thousand in the major leagues were arrested or treated for drug abuse of any kind during that time.

The numbers look equally small in professional football. In 1975 Charles R. Jackson, the assistant director of security for the National Football League, pointed out some figures during a speech to a conference on drug control held in St. Louis, Missouri. Jackson said that of the 8,000 players who had been under contract to the NFL, only thirty had ever been arrested for drug violations during the preceding five-year period. The number arrested added up to less than 0.38 percent of the league's players.

Jackson went on to say that between 1970 and 1975 a total of eighty-six players, or 1.5 percent of the league's

**Len Bias, a promising star of college basketball, died of cocaine abuse at the age of twenty-two.**

athletes, had been linked to drug involvement. Of that number 70 percent had been found not guilty of the drug charges. The thirty drug arrests during the five-year period had involved twenty-nine players, with one player being arrested twice. All things considered, Jackson argued, the NFL's drug problem at the time was being caused by a very small percentage of players.

But Jackson's speech was made in 1975. The greatest increase in cocaine abuse and in drug testing has come in the years since. And so, what is the situation today? Are more players now involved in drug abuse than in earlier years?

Using the National Football League's urine-testing program as a yardstick for most, if not all, professional sports, the answer is that the problem does not seem appreciably larger than in the past. In 1989 *Sports Illustrated* ran a special feature on the league's testing program and reported that the program had turned up scant evidence of illicit substance use by the players.[8]

*SI* reported that in urine checks prior to the 1986 season 6.5 percent of all NFL players tested positive for cocaine, marijuana, alcohol, and assorted other drugs. In the preseason checks for 1987, 9.6 percent tested positive. The magazine then pointed out that most of the positive results were for alcohol and over-the-counter drugs. In preseason 1986 a mere 0.7 percent of the players tested positive for cocaine, and only 0.8 percent in 1987.

*Sports Illustrated* felt that these percentages should have been even lower. The magazine reported that the NFL, whose drug-testing program is acknowledged as one of the toughest in sports, apparently listed players as positive for amounts that would be considered negative elsewhere. For example, *SI* pointed out that in 1988 the National Institute on Drug Abuse (NIDA) established a standard for judging cocaine tests. The standard calls for a test to be designated positive only if the urine sample has at least 150 nanograms of cocaine metabolite in it. (A nanogram equals one-billionth of a gram. A metabolite is a product of metabolism.) The standard was set for the testing of government employees who work in installations (such as nuclear and aviation plants) where the public safety demands a drug-free environment. It was quickly accepted by private industry. But, of the seventeen NFL players who tested positive for cocaine in preseason 1987, six tested below the NIDA mark.

But what of cocaine users among college and high school athletes? There are no precise statistics on their number. But one optimistic point can be made here. Whatever their number, it is thought to be declining through the years, because studies indicate that cocaine use by *all* college and high school students is declining—and has been doing so since 1986. For example, consider the following data from the Institute on Drug Abuse: a 1985 survey showed that 17.3 percent of the students of 135 public and private high school graduating classes admitted to having tried cocaine. In a 1986 survey the percentage dropped to 16.9. Then it went to 15.2 in 1987 and plunged to 12.1 in 1988, the last year to be reported.[9]

The same holds true for crack, the smokable form of cocaine. With a price tag of $5 to $10 per dose, it was marketed in the mid-1980s in an effort to "hook" younger people who could not afford the more expensive drug. But the data from NIDA shows that it has not been all that popular. Of the members of the 135 graduating classes in 1987, 5.6 percent admitted to using the drug. The percentage for 1988 stood at 4.8.

The declining popularity of cocaine among college and high school students and also the general public as the drug's harmful effects become increasingly known is thought to be largely responsible for the fall in its price that was mentioned earlier in the chapter.

Though there is evidence that the number of players in all sports involved in cocaine abuse seems to be small— and though cocaine seems to be slipping in popularity on the college and high school scene—a word of caution is needed here. For a variety of reasons, no one can really say for certain just how extensive the abuse is. Cocaine is an illegal drug and thus is abused in secret. Further, many teams, both professional and collegiate, do not make the results of their drug testing public but handle the matter privately when they must counsel a player for a drug problem or send him to a rehabilitation program. Finally, there are various strategies that can be used to avoid positive test results. If notified in advance of a test, players can turn to other drugs that will mask the one that the test would otherwise reveal. Given twenty-four-hours' warning, they can flush the illegal drug out of their systems by downing quantities of water, cranberry juice, or vinegar mixed with water.

In 1991 fifteen university football players in southern California told the *Los Angeles Times* of still other strategies. They spoke of knowing players who brought in urine from a nonuser and then, when no one was looking, placed it in the test vial and passed it off as their own. There were players, they said, who placed "clean" urine in a container and hid it beneath their clothes; during the test, they seemed to be urinating, but in reality were passing the clean urine down through a tube from its container.[10]

And so, even with the seemingly small number of offenders, the drug problem looms large in the eyes of the National Football League, the National Basketball League, the two baseball leagues, and the National Hockey League. All four have taken action against it. We'll report their actions in Chapter Eleven.

But now let's take a close look at cocaine itself, and then marijuana, to see what each does to the athlete-user.

# 9

# COCAINE AND THE ATHLETE

___

Cocaine is one of eighteen alkaloids found in the leaves of the coca plant. It is, in fact, the major alkaloid present, accounting for about 0.5 to 1.0 percent of each leaf's weight. The drug seems to be nature's way of protecting the leaves from foraging animals. It is quite bitter to the taste.

(Alkaloids are substances present in certain fungi and plants. They consist of various elements, a principal one being nitrogen. They are poisonous, but can serve as powerful medicines when used carefully in small amounts.)

As for the coca plant itself, it can take the shape of either a tree or a bush. In appearance, it resembles somewhat the blackthorn bush of Europe and North America. Despite the resemblance, it grows almost exclusively in South America, both in the lowlands and along the slopes of the Andes Mountains. In general, it rises to a height of about 8 feet (2.5 m), bears long and straight branches, and produces leaves that are colored a bright green on their tops and a pale gray-green on the undersides.

## FROM BUSH TO POWDER

Cocaine is extracted from the leaves after they have been pulled from the plant. They are burned in a mixture of kerosene, sulfuric acid, and an alkali. The drug emerges as a

sticky paste. The paste contains between 70 and 85 percent pure cocaine, with the remainder of the mass being made up of other coca alkaloids, plus some oil from the leaves.

Further processing—done with hydrochloric acid—transforms the paste into white flakes and lumps, both of which can be easily crushed to a fine powder. The powder is known as cocaine hydrochloride. The processing eliminates many of the alkaloids and much of the leaf oil. Left in the powder is a cocaine content ranging from 90 percent to a completely pure 100 percent. The degree of purity largely depends on how well and carefully the processing has been carried out. Of course, the purer the cocaine is, the more potent it is.

As you know, cocaine is an illegal drug in many of the world's nations, the United States among them. But the drug itself is not widely used *everywhere* in the world. It finds its greatest popularity in Europe, Australia, and the Americas—Canada, the United States, Mexico, Central America, the Caribbean islands, and its homeland, South America. It is not widely used in the Middle East, Asia Minor, and Asia itself. In these areas the chief drug of abuse is opium (which comes from the poppy flower of the opium plant and is the base substance for heroin), followed closely by certain types of marijuana, chief among them hashish.

The principal coca-growing countries are Peru and Bolivia. Because of today's massive demand for cocaine, coca cultivation is now under way in Brazil and Colombia.

Once the cocaine gum is obtained by the Peruvian and Bolivian growers, it is sent out of the country for processing into the white powder. Peru and Bolivia are agricultural nations that do not yet have the industrial means to do large-scale processing of cocaine.

**The leaves of the coca plant (top) are harvested and processed (bottom) to yield the powerful drug, cocaine.**

The main processing country is Colombia, a nation that has enriched itself over the years by processing and distributing illegal drugs of all types—from cocaine to marijuana and such chemical substances as the amphetamines. After being processed, cocaine is smuggled to the outside world in various ways—concealed on the persons of air and sea passengers, hidden away among the legitimate freight on airliners and cargo ships, and, especially for those shipments heading to the United States, packed aboard small boats and private airplanes.

The United States stands as one of the world's largest cocaine customers. The U.S. government estimates that from 48 to upward of 50 tons of the drug are smuggled into the country annually. For the most part, cocaine reaches the shores of the United States along the country's southern coast—from Florida on the east to Texas on the west. There are also several major destination points on the Pacific and Atlantic coasts, chief among them Los Angeles and San Francisco in the west, and New York City in the east. Once it has arrived, the drug is shipped throughout the country, again by various means—trucks, trains, and commercial and private airplanes.

## EARLY COCAINE USES

The South Americans early identified cocaine as a valuable medical drug. Its ability to deaden feeling in the tongues of Incas led to its use as an anesthetic in a number of ancient surgical operations.

On the other hand, when it was first introduced into Europe and the United States, in the late nineteenth century, many physicians thought that its energizing effects could be put to use in the treatment of depression. Among them was the famous pioneer in psychoanalysis, Austria's Sigmund Freud. He took the drug himself and administered it to patients in need of having their spirits lifted.

Freud also noted that cocaine, in common with the amphetamines, has the power to curb the appetite. He prescribed it for certain digestive disorders. For a number of years, cocaine was medically employed in weight control.

Today, replaced by other drugs and widely banned in the world as dangerous, cocaine serves little medical purpose. It is pretty much limited to use as a local anesthetic in certain surgeries.

## WHAT COCAINE DOES TO THE BODY

When now reading of how cocaine acts on the body, you may well think that you've turned the pages back to the chapter on the amphetamines. The effects of both drugs are so much alike as to seem identical.

For instance, isn't there a familiar ring to these physical effects? The heartbeat quickens. The body temperature rises. So does the blood pressure. And, as just mentioned, the appetite diminishes.

And what of the greatest of all the cocaine effects—its tremendous thrust of energy? No sooner does cocaine enter the bloodstream than it hits the user with that energy and a sense of well-being that can mount to euphoria. At the same time, there is a flood of self-confidence—the surging belief that the user is better than everyone else and able to handle any work or social situation that may arise.

There is one difference, however, between the cocaine and amphetamine highs. The amphetamine highs, you'll recall, can last from several hours to two or three days. The cocaine-induced energy and self-confidence fade in twenty to thirty minutes and disappear entirely a short time later.

But back to the similarities. The descent from the cocaine high matches that of the amphetamine's return journey. There is great tiredness and often the need to sleep. Especially for the steady user, there can be a frightening sense of depression, one that is frequently accompanied by intense irritability, nervousness, and restlessness.

To overcome the descent problems, longtime users imitate amphetamine victims by taking alcohol, sedatives, Quaaludes, and even heroin to calm themselves. Then, in common with the amphetamine victim, they find themselves in a vicious circle of "uppers and downers." Depressed to the point of being unable to become energetic on their own, they reach for cocaine for the trip to pleasure and confidence; then reach for the "downers" to ease the return to normal; and then reach again for cocaine for another ride up.

## PROLONGED AND HEAVY USE

Pointing out yet another similarity to the amphetamines, recent research indicates that small amounts of cocaine taken at widely separated intervals do no more harm than the light use of alcohol or cigarettes. It is the prolonged and heavy use of the drug that invites trouble.

The trouble matches that caused by undisciplined amphetamine use: insomnia, a deepening depression, paranoid fears and behavior, and hallucinations. Physically, with the appetite perennially curbed, there can be a dangerous weight loss and a lowering of the body's resistance to disease. In time, the liver cells can be harmed. And as more time passes, there can be the increasing danger of a heart attack. However, from the very first days of use, there is the ever-present threat of death from overdose.

And now a final comparison with the amphetamines: As is the case with them, medical science does not yet know for certain whether heavy cocaine use is physically addictive. But like the amphetamines, and for the same reason, cocaine is widely suspected of being psychologically addictive. Many steady and heavy users at last reach the point where they feel unable to function without its help.

Cocaine holds at least two special threats for users, whether they are new to or well acquainted with the drug. The threats are present because of the ways cocaine is taken: by hypodermic injection or inhalation. Hypodermic injection is made possible by the fact that cocaine is soluble in liquid. Inhalation, which is popularly known as "snorting," works in two ways. The user either sniffs the powder up the nose or breathes in the fumes from a heated cocaine solution.

With cocaine being an illegal drug, injection is dangerous because it is usually self-administered. Dirty needles are often used (as is also true with other drugs of abuse). They threaten infection and the chance of passing on a disease carried by a previous user. As for inhalation, it sends the drug to the bloodstream via mucous membranes in the nose. On passing through, the cocaine constricts the blood vessels, reducing the blood supply and drying up the nose. Ulcers can form after a while on the membrane tissues. The nasal septum is then apt to break open and form little holes in one or more spots. The little holes can be closed only with surgery.

## HOW COCAINE WORKS

Even today, doctors are uncertain about how cocaine works to energize the body. A leading theory is that cocaine, like many other stimulant drugs, produces an action on certain body chemicals when it enters the bloodstream. These chemicals are called *neurotransmitters*. The cocaine prompts them to activate the nerve cells and send tiny electrical impulses coursing through the nervous system.

The impulses affect various body functions, such as the heartbeat, and pour in on at least two areas of the brain—the hypothalamus and the cerebral cortex. The hypothalamus controls such physical operations as the body's temperature and such emotions as anger and fear. The cerebral cortex governs a number of our mental activities.

As a result of this invasion of impulses—so the theory goes—the brain turns into something like an overloaded telephone switchboard when all the electrical impulses come pouring in. It simply cannot respond to all the "incoming calls." As a consequence, the body and the brain become overly energized.

As we did with the anabolic steroids and the amphetamines, we come at last to that all-important question: Why have a number of famous and highly paid sports stars, with everything to lose, risked the dangers of cocaine? The answer is to be found in the two roles that cocaine plays in sports—first, as an abused recreational drug and then as a misused winning-edge drug.

## COCAINE'S RECREATIONAL ABUSE

In the world at large, today's cocaine abuse is seen mainly among adults. The reason is that cocaine, to recall a point made earlier, is a highly expensive drug. Though its price tag varies from time to time, with much of the charge depending on the amount of the drug being made available to the illegal market, cocaine usually sells for between $70 and $100 per gram (.035 oz) in the United States. A cocaine habit can cost an American user dearly—say, from around $500 to upwards of $2,000 a week. Prices are just as stiff in Canada and Europe.

Its price tag puts cocaine beyond the financial reach of all but the wealthiest young people. Likewise, its cost is too much for countless adults earning an average wage. Yet, many of them take cocaine on a steady basis and sacrifice any number of life's necessities to satisfy their habit. The drug, however, is most often found among high-income professional people.

Drug authorities think that cocaine is highly popular among the nation's affluent professional people for reasons other than the mere fact that they can afford it. A belief here is that the drug provides relief from the tensions created by high-salaried work and the complex personal and social responsibilities that almost invariably accompany it. Another belief holds that a number of high earners are users because, despite their respected positions and large incomes, they actually have little confidence in themselves or their abilities. They like and need the sense of superiority and the feeling of "being up to anything" that cocaine induces. And, returning to the idea of cost, some authorities say that many users first try cocaine so that they can gain the status that comes of being able to afford so expensive a drug.

The above points can all be easily transferred to the sports world. Cocaine is beyond the financial reach of most amateurs and so is found principally in the professional ranks. As is true of the world at large, it is abused recreationally for reasons quite aside from the fact that the professional players can handle its cost.

Dr. Joseph Pursch of CareUnit Hospitals pointed to one very basic reason in a 1983 issue of *U.S. News & World Report* magazine. He said that many professional players not only have a great deal of money but also plenty of free time on their hands. They spend much of each season uprooted from home and living in hotel rooms. They are often handed drugs by fans and admirers. The slide into a ruinous drug habit for recreational purposes—for just passing the empty and restless hours when not at work—can come all too easily.

There are other reasons just as basic. To understand them, you need only put yourself in the professional's place. There's all that money. There's all that fame. There's all that public adulation. And there are all those constant demands made on you by the team, by the fans, and by yourself. Win. Outperform your opponent so that your salary is justified and your pride maintained. Never let down. Especially never let down because if you do, there's always someone waiting to step in and take over your job.

Again, the slide into a harmful recreational cocaine habit can come all too easily for any number of reasons—all the way from trying to live in the "fast lane" because of your money and fame to forgetting the pressures of your life and feeling, for a few fleeting moments, that you're as heroic as you're supposed to be.

## COCAINE FOR
## THAT WINNING EDGE

There was a time when cocaine use in the sports world was solely for recreational purposes. In recent years, however, things have changed. More and more, cocaine has been tried as a medical drug. Players have turned to it in the hope that its energy will give them that cherished winning edge.

In particular, this change has been observed in professional football. As several sports doctors have pointed out, cocaine's painkilling capability is especially sought for in this game of bruising, crunching body contact. As the player-users see it, the drug, like the amphetamines, enables them to withstand more pain than they could without it. They say they can hit harder and absorb harder hits.

For many players the drug has replaced the amphetamines. The reasons given for the switch are various. The players say that cocaine does not confuse a person's mental faculties to the extent that the amphetamines do. They find the trip back down to normal—at least in the beginning stages of use—easier than it is from an amphetamine high. And, again in the beginning phases of use, cocaine's aftereffects strike them as being less severe than those of the amphetamines.

Some players like the drug because its effects last a shorter time than those of the amphetamines—twenty to thirty minutes as opposed to several hours or even two or three days. They get their high only for the length of time it is really needed and not for long hours after the final gun. One football player has commented that users look on cocaine as a "second-half drug," to be taken when tiredness and the aches of all the continuing hard body contact are at their worst.

News reports have suggested that the misuse of cocaine as a medical drug is also known in baseball, this because of the exceedingly long playing season, which brings on a cumulative sense of tiredness and pain.

But, though the sports use of cocaine as a pleasure or medical drug is highly regrettable and dangerous, this chapter should end on a positive note. Although cocaine's continuing popularity has made it the drug not only of the 1980s but also the 1990s, there are indications that its use in athletics is declining on two fronts. First, as *Sports Illustrated* pointed out in 1989, only a small percentage of NFL players tested positive for cocaine when urine checks were held prior to the 1986 and 1987 seasons. Second, the surveys that were conducted from 1986 through 1988 showed that cocaine use was steadily declining among *all* graduating high school students. It can be taken for granted that many athletes were among their number.

# 10

# MARIJUANA

---

Cocaine may well be called the drug of the 1980s and 1990s because it has been so widely abused. But the fact is that marijuana has been even more widely abused. In the mid-1980s, the federal government estimated that upward of 25 million American adults and young people—approximately 12 percent of the nation's population—were using marijuana on a regular basis, meaning at least once a month. That figure far outstripped the reported 15 to 20 million Americans who have tried cocaine in recent years.

Further, a 1988 survey revealed that around 35 percent of the country's college students had used marijuana within the preceding twelve months. In the same year, a survey of the members of 135 high school graduating classes showed that 47.2 percent of their number admitted to marijuana use. The college figure for cocaine abuse in 1988 hovered at around 10 percent, while the high school percentage stood at 12.1.[1]

Marijuana is especially popular among young people because it is so inexpensive. The drug comes in varying grades of potency, with the charge for better grades running up to about $200 per ounce (28 g). Some lower grades can be bought for between $36 and $60 an ounce. Still lower grades are available at an even cheaper price and can cost the user as little as a few pennies per cigarette. Contrasted with cocaine's sales tag of $70 to $100 for a gram, marijuana costs next to nothing. (The figures given here are general ones. The cost of marijuana, as is true of cocaine, can change, rising or falling from time to time and from area to area.)

Like cocaine, marijuana is outlawed in many parts of the world. In Europe it is illegal in all countries but one, Spain. Its cultivation, sale, and possession are banned throughout the United States. Federal penalties for trafficking in more than 1,000 pounds (454 kg) of the drug can bring a fine of $125,000 and up to fifteen years in prison for a first offense. The fine can jump to $250,000 and the prison sentence to twenty years for a second offense. State marijuana laws vary greatly, with possession of a small amount—perhaps an ounce or two—usually being considered a misdemeanor that can result in a fine of several hundred dollars and/or a jail sentence of a few weeks or months. Major trafficking offenses are apt to earn prison sentences of one year to life.

Despite the nation's antimarijuana laws, about 10,000 to 15,000 tons of the drug are smuggled to American users each year. The tonnage has an estimated value of more than $24 billion. Mostly, the marijuana is brought in from other countries. An increasing amount, however, is being grown within the United States itself.

## DAMAGED CAREERS
## AND REPUTATIONS

Countless Americans have been arrested, imprisoned, or otherwise punished over the years for using and/or selling marijuana. Among those most damaged by their marijuana involvement have been athletes whose reputations easily match those caught in the nation's cocaine scandals.

To name but a few: In 1973, the then NFL commissioner, Pete Rozelle, charged the Los Angeles Rams' brilliant wide receiver, Lance Rentzel, with personal misconduct, including the illegal possession of marijuana, and suspended him from play for the season. The 1980s opened with shock for baseball fans when they heard that catcher Darrell Porter of the Kansas City Royals had gone to a rehabilitation center for treatment of alcoholism and a drug dependency. Revealed was the story of a gifted player who felt so pressured to succeed throughout his life that he had sought escape not only in drink but in marijuana, amphetamines, and eventually cocaine. Shock erupted again in 1984 when running back Chuck Muncie was handed a season's suspension from the NFL after failing a urine test during negotiations that would have sent him from the San Diego Chargers to the Miami Dolphins. The chief chemical in marijuana was detected in his urine. Muncie had twice been treated for drug dependency in 1982.

One of the saddest of all stories belongs to Orlando Cepeda, for seventeen years a superb National League first baseman and hitter. In a career that saw him make up the heart of the San Francisco Giants' batting order (with Willie Mays and Willy McCovey) and take the St. Louis Cardinals to the 1967 World Series, Cepeda amassed a splendid record—more than 2,100 games, 2,351 hits, 379 home runs, and 1,365 runs batted in (RBI). In 1961 he led the league in both home runs (46) and RBI (142). For leading the Cardinals to the World Series with a .325 batting average, 25 home runs, and 111 RBI, Cepeda was named 1967's Most Valuable Player in the National League.

When he retired, he did so as a national hero, both in the mainland United States and his homeland, Puerto Rico. But then came a day in 1978 at Puerto Rico's San Juan airport. Cepeda and a friend walked into the freight terminal and collected a box sent to them from Colombia. Police and drug agents closed in on the pair and took possession of the crate. On being opened, it was found to contain 165 pounds (75 kg) of marijuana worth about $66,000.

Arrested and charged with importing and possessing marijuana, Cepeda was sentenced to five years in prison. He served only nine months of the term, but has been paying heavily in lost reputation ever since. Along with the late Roberto Clemente, he was once the pride of Puerto

**Orlando Cepeda's arrest for marijuana
possession cost him public respect and—perhaps—
election to the Baseball Hall of Fame.**

Rico. Further, he came from the island's most respected baseball family; his father had been known as the Babe Ruth of Puerto Rico. For years, Cepeda was the target of scorn and anger there. It was as if the people felt that his drug involvement had betrayed the whole commonwealth after bringing them such honor. Cepeda once told a reporter that he thought his people would never forgive him for what he had done.

In 1990 another member of the San Francisco Giants made sports headlines when the team announced that outfielder Rick Leach was being suspended from the lineup and major-league baseball for sixty days following a test that showed the presence of "an illegal substance" in his system.[2] The Giants' management declined to reveal what substance had been detected, but the press suspected it to be marijuana. This suspicion stemmed from the fact that when Leach was a member of the Texas Rangers in 1989 he had mysteriously disappeared for thirty-six hours. The police had been informed and had entered his hotel room in their efforts to locate him. There they came upon what they called "a small amount" of marijuana.

At the time of his suspension Leach issued this statement: "I know I have disappointed my family, my teammates, and the Giants. . . . I'm sorry for letting them down, and I hope I can get this behind me so that I can get back to playing." He then voluntarily entered a drug rehabilitation program, and there was great hope that he would be successful.

## WHAT IS MARIJUANA?

Marijuana is one of the names given to the chemicals in a yellowish resin found in the hemp plant. Known in botany as the *Cannabis sativa L*, the plant thrives in temperate and tropical climates and thus can be found in wide-ranging areas of the world. It grows in Asia—in China, Japan, and Korea, and westward from India to Lebanon. It is to be found in such European countries as France, Hungary, Italy, and Yugoslavia. In the Western Hemisphere the growing areas are located in Central and South America, Mexico,

and the United States. The plant seems able to thrive almost anywhere in the United States. The heaviest domestic cultivation is reported to take place in Hawaii, California, Oregon, North Carolina, and West Virginia.

The plant usually grows to a height of 10 to 20 feet (3 to 6 m). It sprouts long, flowering branches which, in their turn, sprout leaves that run from 3 to 10 inches (8 to 25 cm) long. Both the male and female hemp plants contain some sixty-one chemicals, with one—tetrahydrocannabinol ($\Delta$-9-THC)—being the chief source of intoxication. The male plant, however, contains but a small THC content. The female plant is responsible for the major share of the world's marijuana supply.

The drug is obtained from the upper parts of the plant—from its stems, flowers, flower seeds, and leaves. Marijuana, as mentioned earlier, comes in various strengths. Those strengths are determined by the amount of THC produced in individual plants or plant strains. The most potent marijuanas are bhang, ghanga, and hashish. They are cultivated mainly in Asia.

For marketing, the plant's resinous parts are crushed into a greenish tobaccolike substance. The drug is then usually smoked, in a pipe or as a cigarette. It may also be mixed in food or liquid. One of marijuana's many nicknames, tea, springs from the early Asian practice of mixing the drug in various brews, chief among them tea. Among its other nicknames are pot, grass, weed, and Mary Jane.

The hemp plant has been helping the world since ancient times. From it has come a tough fiber that has gone into the manufacture of rope, clothing, ship's caulking, sacking, and paper. Historians believe the plant originated in Asia, in an area north of the Himalayas. They know that the Chinese were cultivating the plant for its fibers as early

**The hemp plant (top) is processed into the illegal drug marijuana (bottom), being gathered up by a police officer after a drug bust.**

as 2800 B.C. They theorize it made its way west to Europe in about A.D. 500. It traveled farther westward with the early American colonists.

The *Cannabis sativa L* continues to be of economic service today. Its fiber is used in the production of rope. Its seeds go into the manufacture of paints and varnishes.

As for marijuana itself, it, too, has been known since ancient times. It was early put to work in medicine, in great part because of its ability to induce a state of dreamy relaxation in the user. Shen Nung, the Chinese emperor whose studies 4,000 years ago opened the way to the modern development of the amphetamines, also investigated the cannabis plant and said that its resin could be of value in the relief of such varied problems as emotional upset, constipation, gout, beriberi, and even absentmindedness. A number of ancient cultures, among them that of India, used the drug's relaxing effects to treat nervousness and depression.

Western medicine learned about marijuana in the early nineteenth century. For the remainder of the century, it was sought for the treatment of various physical and psychological complaints, depression being a chief representative of the latter. In our century, marijuana has been replaced by other medical drugs and is rarely employed for the ill, especially in the Western world. At present, however, one marijuana drug—delta 9 tetrahydrocannabinol—is under medical study. A laboratory-produced drug derived from marijuana's chief chemical, it is being researched for possible work in controlling the nausea and vomiting triggered by the chemotherapy treatments given cancer patients. The synthesized drug is also being considered as an agent for reducing the within-the-eye pressure that marks the presence of glaucoma, a disorder that, if not controlled, leads to blindness.

## THE MARIJUANA HIGH

Marijuana hits the user in much the same way as alcohol. It interferes with the smooth functioning of the brain and brings on a state of intoxication. But it is an intoxication that differs from the drunkenness of alcohol in a very basic manner.

Drunkenness can affect a person in various ways—from a silly happiness to an equally silly sadness to an intense and even dangerous anger. Marijuana intoxication—the drug's high—usually follows a set pattern and ends in a specific way. To begin, there is a feeling of restlessness. Next, there is a growing sense of well-being. The user than enters the dreamy state of relaxation that was mentioned earlier.

A number of physical reactions occur as the pattern develops. The blood pressure goes up. The heartbeat quickens. The pupils of the eyes dilate. The flow of saliva drops, often bringing on a sudden thirst. The thirst is usually for water rather than alcohol, juices or soft drinks. Just as often, there is a sudden hunger.

Marijuana is classified as a hallucinogen (a drug that causes the user to hallucinate) because of some specific effects that may be encountered as the high progresses. For one, a person's vision may distort and cause surrounding objects to assume strange shapes and sparkling colors. Likewise, one's hearing may begin to misbehave. Commonly, the user "hears" bells ring and buzzers go off. The human voice often sounds unreal, as though echoing out of a barrel or coming from a great distance. One's sense of time is also often affected, with everything lapsing into slow motion so that seconds seem like long minutes.

Small amounts of marijuana trigger these visual and auditory tricks. Full hallucinations—the "seeing" of things that aren't there—arrive with heavier amounts. As is true of the amphetamines and cocaine dosages, a very heavy intake of marijuana can induce toxic psychosis, with the victim hallucinating wildy and "seeing" imaginary bugs everywhere.

The hallucinations sound frightening. But not the drug's other effects, mainly that dreamy state of relaxation. They, in fact, sound pleasant. But there is evidence to show that they are sometimes anything but pleasant. Users have reported sudden feelings of restlessness, fear, and physical upset during highs. One user, for example, recalled that his head seemed to have turned into a balloon and was ready to burst at any moment.

To date, drug studies have not settled the question of whether marijuana is physically addictive. But the drug is widely thought to be psychologically addictive. The belief here is that in time habitual users cannot relax and put aside life's burdens for a time without marijuana.

There is also the belief that long-term abuse alters an individual's view of life in a negative way. Such qualities as self-esteem, personal ambition, and desire to succeed are reportedly blunted. The change in personality resulting from long use of marijuana interferes with the user's overall ability to function successfully in the everyday world.

As for long-term physical damage, physicians point out that marijuana is usually smoked. Therefore, it poses the same dangers to the lungs and heart as does tobacco.

## MARIJUANA IN SPORTS

Unlike cocaine, marijuana plays just one role in sports. It is abused in the search for pleasure and relaxation or as a means of escaping from reality for a time. It is not used as a winning-edge drug.

The reason is obvious. The state of dreaminess produced by its high renders marijuana useless as a winning-edge drug. The user moves slowly and clumsily. Reaction time slows and the hands lose their steadiness. Good perception goes out the window on account of all those visual tricks being played by the drug. In short, the user has neither the mental sharpness nor the physical agility to be anything but helpless in the hands of an alert opponent.

In two ways, however, a number of athletes use marijuana as if it were, at least in part, a winning-edge drug.

First, as you know, some turn to it on the trip down from an amphetamine or cocaine high, easing the journey downward so that they can recover all the more quickly for their next competition date. And some use marijuana to relax prior to competition, usually taking the drug during the preceding evening for a good night's sleep. Doctors say that the sleep is apt to do no good. The user often awakens feeling unwell, as though suffering an alcoholic hangover.

There are strong indications that marijuana, like cocaine, has been losing its popularity among both professional and amateur athletes over the past few years.

In Chapter Eight we spoke of the 1989 *Sports Illustrated* report on the National Football League's annual preseason urine-testing program. We limited ourselves in the chapter to the league's cocaine findings. We turn now to what the program revealed about the players' use of marijuana.[3]

In the urine check prior to the 1986 season, 1.8 percent of the players tested positive for the drug. The figure dropped slightly to 1.6 percent in the preseason 1987 checks.

*Sports Illustrated,* as it did with the league's cocaine findings, felt that the marijuana percentages might have been too high. Widely accepted at the time was the belief that a marijuana metabolite level of 50 nanograms or less in the body adds up to what is called "passive inhalation"— the amount of smoke that someone might breathe in from another's marijuana cigarette at, say, a party. It does not necessarily mean that the test subject is a user. Yet, according to league data seen by *SI,* forty-one players tested positive for marijuana in preseason 1987; of their number, thirty-four had test readings below the 50-nanogram mark.

You'll recall from Chapter Eight that in 1988 the National Institute on Drug Abuse (NIDA) set a minimum level of nanograms that have to be present in the system for government workers to test positive for cocaine use. At the same time the NIDA established a level of 15 nanograms of marijuana metabolite as being necessary for a marijuana test to be judged positive. Had the NIDA standard been in effect in 1987, ten of the forty-one players who tested positive in the preseason check that year would have been below the Institute's new level.

The NFL's findings did more than reveal a dip in marijuana use between 1986 and 1987. The low percentage of positive tests also indicated that the drug was little used by the players. If football players are representative of the competitors in all types of professional sports, then it might be said that marijuana attracts very few athletes throughout the pro ranks. But this is a dangerous conclusion to reach because no one knows for certain exactly how many professional players use the drug. Marijuana is an illegal substance and thus is abused in secret. Many teams do not make public the results of their testing programs, but prefer to handle matters with a troubled player privately. Finally, there are ways to flush an illegal drug out of one's system before a test or to mask its presence with legal drugs.

More indicative of marijuana's waning popularity are statistics derived from surveys of college and high school students. As mentioned at the start of this chapter, a 1988 survey showed that 35 percent of college students and 47.2 percent of the members of 135 high school graduating classes admitted to having used marijuana.[4] These percentages, which were reported by the National Institute on Drug Abuse, are alarmingly high. But alarming as they are, both show a sharp decline in marijuana abuse over the past years. For example, the NIDA said that the number of college users was down 15 points from the 50 percent that was reported in 1980. Further, the percentage of college and high school students who used marijuana daily had dropped from 10.7 in 1978 to 2.7 in 1988. Still further, in 1978 35 percent of the young people surveyed thought there was a great risk involved in the regular use of marijuana; that number had vaulted more than 40 points to 77 percent by 1988.

On a year-to-year basis the survey of the graduating high school classes (from both public and private schools) best shows the drug's steady loss of popularity. The survey was taken annually throughout the 1980s, with 1988 being the last year for which figures are available. Though graduating high school seniors of all types were involved, it must be assumed that a good number of athletes were among them. The results of the survey show the following diminishing percentages of marijuana use:

**1980 = 60.3 percent**
**1981 = 59.5 percent**
**1982 = no figure given**

**1983 = 57.0 percent**
**1984 = 54.9 percent**
**1985 = 54.2 percent**
**1986 = 50.9 percent**
**1987 = 50.2 percent**
**1988 = 47.2 percent**
Source: *The World Almanac and Book of Facts: 1990*, p. 171.

It is felt that the growing public awareness of marijuana's dangers—through press reports, educational programs, and the personal experiences of users—is greatly responsible for the decline in its use.

We've now come to the end of our look at the drugs found in sports. Now we're ready for the last of the five questions that were asked in Chapter One:

What is the sports world doing to curb or end its problems of drug use and abuse?

# 11

## WORKING TO STOP
## THE PROBLEM

---

The sports world is working on five fronts to curb and perhaps one day end its problems with drugs. Those five fronts are: drug testing, monitoring, education, rehabilitation, and disciplinary action. All five are blended together in various drug-prevention programs, but they can be discussed individually.

### DRUG TESTING:
### IN AMATEUR SPORTS

For more than twenty years, major amateur competitions in such sports as weight lifting, cycling, and track and field have been employing measures to detect the presence of drugs in athletes. They have done so through the use of saliva and urine tests. When the tests reveal the presence of a forbidden drug in an athlete's system, the competitor may be banned from the competition or deprived of his or her victory medals.

One of the most stringent of all drug-testing programs is carried out at the Olympic Games. Olympic officials began testing for drugs in 1967. At the time, they were principally interested in such winning-edge drugs as the amphetamines, but added the anabolic steroids to their list of forbidden substances in 1973. In recent years more than 300 drugs have been banned by the Games.

To see just how stringent the Olympic testing program is, we need only look at the procedures used in the 1984 and 1988 Games. In both years an Olympics representative was assigned to each event. Immediately after any event, the representative summoned the first-, second-, and third-place winners, along with another competitor picked at random. They were escorted to a nearby drug-testing station, or, as it was widely called, a doping control station. There each athlete gave two samples of urine.

One sample was stored away under strict security in case it would be needed later. The second went to a laboratory maintained by the International Olympic Committee, there to be tested. If the test proved negative—if no forbidden substance revealed itself—all was well. But if the result came up positive, a medical committee immediately informed the athlete and his or her team officials of the finding.

A second analysis was then carried out in the presence of International Olympic Committee representatives and officials from the athlete's team. If it, too, proved positive, the athlete was stripped of his or her medals.

Similarly tough testing measures are employed in such major competitions as the Pan American Games and the various European championships. Testing in the United States is performed in many national, state, and regional amateur events.

For example, the National Collegiate Athletic Association (NCAA) has long tested competitors appearing in championship meets. In 1990, however, the NCAA passed a new ruling aimed at the members of major university football teams.[1] The ruling calls for the year-round random testing of players. "Random testing" means that the athletes can be tested at any time without prior warning. The testing is primarily aimed at discovering the presence in a competitor's system of such performance enhancing drugs as the anabolic steroids. In great part the ruling came about

as a result of press reports that the steroids were being widely used by some college athletes.

Under the new ruling a first positive test for a winning-edge drug brings the loss of a year's eligibility for a player. (The same holds true for the discovery of a so-called pleasure drug, such as cocaine or marijuana.) A second positive test for a performance enhancer usually results in the banning of a player from athletics at schools that hold a membership in the NCAA.

As was pointed out above, the new ruling applies only to football players at major universities, players in what is known as Division 1 football. Players in other sports will continue to be tested only when participating in championship meets. In addition to the random testing, all football players will continue to be tested when they appear in bowl games or similar championship competitions.

## DRUG TESTING:
## IN PROFESSIONAL SPORTS

Urine testing has long been a subject of heated controversy in professional sports. It is favored by some in the pro ranks and opposed by others. Those in favor of the testing feel that it is necessary to help control and perhaps eradicate the drug problems found in professional athletics. At the core of the opposition are several beliefs—that testing is too costly and time consuming, that it is impossible to enforce because of player opposition, and that it is unnecessary because the antidrug programs long sponsored by the various leagues are proving successful without it. Many players view the tests as an invasion of privacy and an unnecessary burden.

**A lab technician performs drug tests on urine samples from athletes competing in the 1988 Olympics.**

The National Football League is the only major professional sports organization that administers drug tests to all its players. It has been doing so since 1982.

There are two basic parts to the league's testing program, which is considered one of the toughest in all sports. First, any player who produces a positive test becomes subject to what is called "reasonable cause testing." This means that the league can call for unannounced tests at any time, either in or out of season, if it has reasonable cause to think that the player is still troubled with his problem.

Second, any player who produces two positive tests is required to attend a thirty-day rehabilitation program. The same goes for a player who tests positive once and then becomes involved in a drug incident, such as an arrest for possession or selling. All this also holds true for a player who is involved in two drug incidents.

The league has long wanted to hold random tests for all its players. But it has been prevented from doing so by the NFL Players Association (the players' union). The Association holds that random testing would constitute a violation of the right of privacy held by all the players.

Professional baseball does not conduct a testing program for its major-league players. They are not tested because their representative group, the Players' Association, argues that it is an invasion of privacy. In 1984, however, the Association and the Major League Baseball Player Relations Committee (representing management) reached an agreement that contains provisions for testing major leaguers in certain circumstances. The agreement, which deals with all aspects of how players with drug problems are to be treated medically and/or disciplined, permits a recommendation for testing when a player is under drug treatment or is charged with a drug problem by his team. The recommendation cannot come from the team, but only from a special committee assigned to study all such cases. Called the Joint Review Council, the committee is made up of three members who are "neutral" in the case and who should have special professional knowledge of drugs and experience in combating people's drug abuse problems.

# THE LEAGUE DRUG PROGRAMS: THE EARLY DAYS

By the dawn of the 1970s today's drug problem was widespread among the public and was fast gaining ground in the sports world. At the time, the drugs causing the greatest alarm in athletics were the amphetamines, soon to be joined by the anabolic steroids. As you'll recall from Chapter Five, the amphetamines, even though they had required a doctor's prescription since soon after World War II, were being freely dispensed in professional locker rooms because their dangers were not yet fully appreciated and because their use was not yet sternly curtailed by the federal government. Then came the government's Comprehensive Drug Abuse Prevention and Control Act in 1970 and with it the requirement that the prescribing of the amphetamines be very strictly regulated.

An example of what was first done in professional sports in response to the alarm and the Act comes from baseball. In December 1970 the Association of Professional Baseball Physicians met to discuss the use of drugs in athletics and issued a statement condemning the use of any stimulant that was taken to improve performance. In less than a month, the then commissioner of baseball, Bowie Kuhn, called for a study of drug usage in the pro game. A later report from the commissioner's office (1973) said the study found baseball to be "largely free of drug problems." The report, however, went on to say that, because of the overall public drug abuse—especially by young people—it was felt that a continuing antidrug program should be launched to protect the game in the future.

The commissioner's office was particularly concerned about the drug problems of many of the young players who would be entering the professional ranks in the coming years. The report said that "approximately 500 young men come into professional baseball for the first time each year."

Accordingly, the beginning of an antidrug campaign—called Baseball's Drug Education and Prevention Program—began to take shape. The report by the commissioner's office said that "baseball was the first professional sports organization to adopt such a program" and then went on to explain that three seminars were held during spring training in 1971. Attending were administrative personnel from all the major-league clubs, managers, coaches, and player representatives. They were briefed on the program and on the dangers that drugs posed for professional sports. From there, word of the program went out to all major- and minor-league personnel.

Baseball may have been the first sport to adopt an antidrug program in response to the new government regulations, but professional football was just as active in 1971. The National Football League adopted what came to be called its Drug Control Program. The National Basketball Association launched a program of its own, while the National Hockey League established a strict antidrug policy. The leagues have resembled each other in their efforts. They have all sought to combat the drug problem through the use of four methods. Some leagues have employed all four methods. Others have used fewer. The methods are monitoring, education, rehabilitation, and disciplinary action.

## DRUG MONITORING

The practice of "drug monitoring" is used with the winning-edge medical drugs that can be legally used with a doctor's prescription. It allows the sports organizations to keep close track of how such drugs are dispensed and in what amounts. But just how do the groups get the job done? The National Basketball Association and the National Football League provide two representative examples.

To oversee its antidrug program, the National Basketball Association employs a physician who is an expert in drug matters. The teams provide him with complete inventories of their prescription-drug supplies. He checks the inventories before and throughout the season. The inventories enable him to judge whether team physicians are authorizing the drugs in normal or excessive amounts. Whenever a player receives a prescription drug, a notation is made of it in his medical file. The notation specifies the date of the prescription, the dosage, the doctor's name, and the reason for the prescription.

In the National Football League, the office of the commissioner requires each team to keep a detailed record of all the prescription drugs on hand throughout the season. Each team must submit this record to the commissioner's office at both the beginning and end of the season, with the first due by July 15 and the second by the following January 16. Also, each team must present a monthly record of the prescription drugs purchased throughout the year. The operating head of each team is responsible for submitting the records. As in the NBA, the doctor in charge of the league's drug program is able to judge whether any team is prescribing the drugs to excess.

Further, the players are required to inform their teams of any prescription drugs obtained from outside sources, regardless of whether the medications are given for a minor complaint or in the wake of serious surgery.

When the records, or when reports from other sources— say, from players troubled by the misuse around them— indicate a team's excessive use, the commissioner may take any of a number of steps. These range from investigating the matter and warning the team, to calling for strong disciplinary action. One of the toughest disciplinary actions to date was leveled against the San Diego Chargers in 1974.

That year the office of the then commissioner, Pete Rozelle, heard complaints from several players that amphetamines had been overprescribed for the Chargers during the 1973 season. An investigation proved to his satisfaction that one of the team doctors had prescribed the drugs in excess for eight players between August 2 and November 6, 1973. The investigation ended with disciplinary actions in the form of fines.

The Charger team was fined $20,000 for failing to supervise its administrative personnel. General Manager Harland Svare received a fine of $5,000 for failing to exercise proper supervisory controls over his players and staff. The eight players involved in the scandal were handed fines ranging from $1,000 to $3,000. In total, the fines came to $40,000. The doctor who had overprescribed the amphetamines was discharged.

## DRUG EDUCATION

Drug education in the league programs is aimed at two targets—the team personnel (not only players but also trainers and all other personnel) and the general public.

To reach the two targets, the leagues have engaged in a wide variety of activities over the years. A firm idea of how various those activities are, can be had by looking at a representative few. Here are some examples of the work that has been done with team personnel in baseball and football:

**1971** ☐ Soon after Commissioner Bowie Kuhn holds three seminars to inform managers and staffs of baseball's new antidrug program, a booklet goes out to everyone in organized ball. Titled *Baseball Vs. Drugs*, it has been checked for accuracy by the Federal Bureau of Narcotics and Dangerous Drugs. The booklet describes the baseball antidrug program.

**1972** ☐ Commissioner Kuhn's office prepares a thirty-minute color film on drugs and their dangers. It is distributed to all teams for viewing by their personnel. The teams also make the film available for showings to high schools, colleges, and community groups.

**1972** ☐ Drug authorities are invited to speak to sixteen National Football League teams during the training and regular seasons. Nine clubs have their team physicians speak to the players. Other teams bring in physicians from nearby universities, plus representatives of state and local law enforcement and drug agencies.

**1972** ☐ The NFL sends representatives from each of its clubs to a drug abuse educational course at Washington, D.C. Conducted by the White House Special Action Office for Drug Abuse Prevention, the course lasts three days. The representatives take the information gathered there back to their teams.

**1981** □ Recognizing the difficulties in identifying the players with drug problems because they often keep them a secret and deny their presence, the NFL employs former Minnesota Viking star Carl Eller to serve as a part-time consultant to the league. His job: to meet with team coaches and administrators and point out the signs of drug misuse or abuse. He also works with a number of players. Eller is himself a man who overcame a former drug problem.

**1982** □ Concerned by reports of the growing sports misuse of the anabolic steroids, Commissioner Rozelle sends a letter to all NFL players reminding them of the league's attitude toward the steroids. He writes: "The League recognizes that in certain circumstances physicians may prescribe anabolic steroids for valid medical reasons. However, if these drugs or similar compounds are taken by otherwise healthy players . . . with the intent merely to achieve increased body bulk, strength, stamina, or similar physical and athletic attributes, such actions will be deemed a misuse and will be dealt with under the provision in each player's contract which prohibits 'stimulants or other drugs . . . to enhance on-field performance.' " Mr. Rozelle then comments on the steroid risks uncovered by research.

**1983** □ NFL coaches attend a workshop on drug dependency held at the Betty Ford Center at the Eisenhower Medical Center in Rancho Mirage, California. The workshop's aim is to help the coaches discover drug problems in players and other team personnel.

Similar work has been done in the National Basketball Association. At annual meetings, team physicians, general managers, coaches, trainers, and players are informed of the latest findings in drug research, with steps then being urged to acquaint all association personnel with the dangers of drugs. The doctor in charge of the NBA drug program periodically conducts seminars for all personnel. He is also available to everyone for advice and consultation. Booklets and pamphlets on drug abuse are made available throughout the NBA.

When the drug education programs are directed to the public, they are aimed in great part at the nation's young people. Again, the activities are widely varied. And, again turning to pro football and baseball, here are some examples of what has been done:

**1971** □ The NFL begins a cooperative effort with three government agencies to produce a series of antidrug spot announcements for airing during telecasts of league games. Fifty-eight players appear in the spots. An estimated 1 billion fans view the presentations. Twenty-six players appear in the following year, reaching a cumulative audience estimated at 2 billion. They urge volunteers to step forward and help to combat drug abuse and other social ills. The three government agencies are the National Clearinghouse for Drug Abuse Information, the National Center for Voluntary Action, and the Justice Department's Bureau of Narcotics and Drugs.

**1971** □ At the request of President Richard Nixon, all major league baseball clubs participate in October's National Drug Abuse Prevention Week. Sixty-two players present radio and television spot announcements during the World Series and also make personal appearances at various functions connected with the week. An estimated audience of 140 million see or hear the announcements. For their work, Commissioner Kuhn and the sixty-two players receive certificates of appreciation from President Richard Nixon.

**1972** □ The Dallas Cowboys distribute over 30,000 antidrug posters to the twenty-six junior high schools in their area. They do so through a series of school assemblies that feature a film or an appearance by a Cowboy player, a former addict, a drug enforcement officer, or a physician. The Cowboys produce an additional 100,000 posters for national distribution.

**1975** □ A twenty-page booklet entitled *Drugs in the Game of Life* is prepared for distribution at Super Bowl IX. It is inserted into the 100,000 copies of the game's program. The booklet contains information about the Comprehensive Drug Abuse Prevention and Control Act, penalties for possession of drugs, and facts about the various abused drugs. The NFL prints additional copies of the booklet and makes them available to high schools, colleges, and community groups.

**1984** □ Representatives from baseball, football, basketball, and other sports groups join the National High School Athletic Coaches Association and the federal Drug Enforcement Agency in a drug abuse prevention program. The program is aimed at over 5 million student athletes in some 20,000 high schools.

The latter years of the 1980s and now the opening years of the 1990s have seen numerous stars from all the professional leagues appear in television spots to warn young people against drug abuse and to point out its dangers. The spots have appeared mainly during the telecasts of professional games.

The professional sports leagues are not the only organizations involved in antidrug campaigns. Much activity also takes place at the amateur level. In addition to the work done by the National High School Athletic Coaches Association, community organizations and schools across the nation sponsor drug prevention projects, with the schools also providing much classroom instruction in the subject. For many years the National Collegiate Athletic Association has made a booklet on drug abuse available to coaches and athletes.

## REHABILITATION

Both the amateur and professional leagues take a sympathetic view of players with drug problems. Long prevailing has been the view that the players are troubled with a diseaselike problem. The idea has been to help them through counseling and medical treatment rather than punishment.

To this end, the professional leagues sponsor recovery programs. They bring in physicians, drug experts, and former users to work directly with troubled players. They send the most troubled players to rehabilitation centers for treatment. The treatment—at least, on the player's first trip to a center—and the care that must often follow it are paid for by the leagues. One of the best of these programs is sponsored by the National Football League.

For a number of years the NFL teams usually sent drug cases to nationally known centers such as the CareUnit Hospitals or the Hazelden Foundation, which is located at Center City, Minnesota. But in 1982 Commissioner Rozelle urged a change. Saying that the centers were often too far away from a team's home city to be convenient for either the team or the player, he urged each club to locate a center in its home area. He further asked that each club retain a local physician who is an expert in drug matters and who would be quickly available for advice and assistance. Since then, though the Hazelden Foundation continues to be used, his suggestion has been put into effect throughout the league.

In addition to sponsoring rehabilitation efforts, the leagues depend on the doctors in charge of their programs for help. The physicians at the head of the NBA, NFL, and baseball programs are readily available for consultations with the teams and individual players. The NBA maintains a telephone hotline for use by any player seeking advice or faced with a drug crisis.

## DISCIPLINARY ACTIONS

Though the professional sports leagues are sympathetic toward the drug-troubled player, there has been a toughening of their outlook since the early to mid-1980s. The toughness is directed not at first-time cases, but at users who cannot rid themselves of their problem after treatment or long-term counseling. There is a growing tendency to discipline continued misuse and abuse through fines and suspensions.

Hitherto, such fines and suspensions were limited to players whose abuses got them into trouble with the law, as was the case in the 1983 suspensions of the Washington Redskins' Tony Peters, the St. Louis Cardinals' E. J. Junior, the New Orleans Saints' Greg Stemrick, and the Cincinnati Bengals' Ross Browner and Pete Johnson (see Chapter Eight). Five years earlier, defensemen Don Reese and Randy Crowder of the Miami Dolphins had been suspended from the NFL on being found guilty of trafficking in drugs. After serving one-year prison terms, they were ruled eligible to reenter the League on the provision that each contribute $5,000 of his first year's salary to a Florida drug rehabilitation center.

The 1980s, however, were marked by such cases as those of pitcher Steve Howe and running back Chuck Muncie. Commissioner Bowie Kuhn, as you'll recall from Chapter Eight, fined Howe the equivalent of thirty days' pay—$54,000—when the pitcher went to a rehabilitation center for the second time in two months. In 1984 Muncie was ordered to undergo drug evaluation and comply with any prescribed treatment—or be suspended from play.

The toughening attitude stems from two sources. The first is the spread of cocaine misuse and abuse seen in recent years in the professional ranks. The various leagues fear that it will severely damage the reputations of their games and that countless shocked fans will soon be unwilling to come out and watch, as one football official has put it, "a bunch of millionaire coke heads trying to do their thing." Equally great is the fear that player-users might try to pay off their debts to their dealers by throwing games or giving the dealers a gambling edge by informing them of team injuries.

Second, there is a feeling that rehabilitation centers, while helpful, are not the complete answer to a player's drug problem. Most center treatments last about four weeks and are usually followed by an indeterminate period of postcare and counseling at the player's home base. Four weeks or so of actual treatment cannot be expected to cure a long-standing and deeply embedded habit—unless the patient tries to help himself. The leagues seem to feel that they cannot go on returning him to the centers indefinitely. Sooner or later, he must take the responsibility to help himself.

The only other answer, then, seems to be to discipline continuing users and hope that it helps awaken them to what they must do for themselves. This attitude can be seen in the National Football League's two-part testing program. A player can be suspended from play when he undergoes rehabilitation after two positive drug tests, two drug incidents, or a combination of a positive drug test and an incident. Continued abuse can see players "banned for life," a fate that befell seven NFL stars in 1990. A player so banned can reapply for admission to the league at the end of a year's time.

The new toughness has prompted the baseball leagues to adopt an approach that has been nicknamed the "three strikes and you're out" policy. Under the policy, for his first known drug offense—his "first strike"—a player is warned that he is in trouble with his league and usually submits to counseling or rehabilitation. A second offense brings a temporary suspension from play (from thirty to sixty or more days) and the requirement to undergo rehabilitation treatment. His third and final offense results in his banishment from the game for life. The player may apply for readmission at a later date.[2]

One of the strictest—and undoubtedly the simplest—of drug policies is enforced in the National Hockey League. This policy was firmly stated by league president John Ziegler: "Any player presently in the NHL or who may hereafter join the NHL must face the fact that if he wishes to be involved in illegal drugs then he will, if discovered, lose his privilege of playing in the NHL."

The statement was made immediately after President Ziegler had suspended Don Murdoch of the New York Rangers from play for one season because of drug possession. Since then, the NHL has suffered but a handful of drug cases. In 1983 defenseman Ric Nattress of the Montreal Canadiens was given a season's suspension for the possession of illegal drugs, a suspension that was eventually

**The National Hockey League enforces
a strict policy on drugs. Ric Nattress of
the Montreal Canadiens was suspended in
1983 for possession of an illegal substance.**

reduced to thirty games. The earlier Murdoch suspension had been reduced to forty games.

Bob Probert of the Detroit Red Wings was arrested in March 1989 when 14 grams (a half ounce) of cocaine were found in his possession as he attempted to cross the Canadian border. Ziegler expelled him from the league indefinitely. The player was sentenced to three months' imprisonment and was released in February 1990, after which he faced probation for three years. The NHL allowed him to rejoin his team in March that year, on the first anniversary of his suspension. [3]

In September 1990 the Edmonton Oilers' goalie, Grant Fuhr, was suspended from league play for one year when he admitted to the use of cocaine. He was reinstated five months later, in February 1991. [4]

The tough attitude of the professional leagues toward drugs is causing controversy in the sports world. It is an attitude supported by many nonuser-players. They have grown tired of the behavior and problems of users who seem unable or unwilling to help themselves and who are, in one player's words, "giving the rest of us and the game a bad name." On the other hand, the tough approach has brought the leagues under much critical fire.

For instance, *The Sporting News* in 1990 contended that the NHL's suspension of goalie Grant Fuhr was too harsh because he had not been found with drugs in his possession but had admitted to a cocaine problem and, on the advice of his agent, had undergone rehabilitation treatment. [5] Seven years earlier, in 1983, *Sports Illustrated* severely criticized the heavy fine imposed on baseball's Steve Howe. Both publications claimed that such punishments would drive athletes' misuse and abuse of drugs underground and discourage many players from stepping forth, admitting their problem, and asking for help.

*Sports Illustrated* has also had some unkind words for the National Football League's testing program. In 1989 *SI* contended that the league's extremely tough attitude (its habit, for instance, of declaring a marijuana test positive when it reveals no more than a "passive inhalation" amount of the drug) is largely meant for public relations reasons—to demonstrate that the league is out to get offenders at all costs. *SI* went on to report that many players think the league "plays favorites" in regard to some of its stars, warning them in advance of test dates. The magazine cited the case of one player—now retired and a potential candidate for the Hall of Fame—whose positive test for cocaine in 1987 was ignored by the league.[6]

## A FINAL NOTE

Can testing, monitoring, education and rehabilitation programs, and disciplinary actions curb—or perhaps even end—the misuse and abuse of drugs in both amateur and professional sports?

At the moment, there is no way of telling. Often the measures seem to be succeeding. Often they seem to be failing. But whatever the successes and failures may be, the misuse and abuse continue to spread through the sports world at all levels. More than one player and coach has likened the spread to a cancer. Only time can tell when and how the cure will come, as assuredly it must if sports are not to be irreversibly harmed.

In the eyes of many athletes and fans, the cure can come only if the above measures are joined by a new public attitude toward sports. They feel that athletics have become competitive in all the wrong ways during the latter half of this century. The accent has been too much on victory—so much so that it has become victory at any cost. At both the amateur and professional levels, the winners are over-idolized and the losers overscorned. At the professional level the athletes are made into highly paid warriors, with the pay rising higher and higher with their every win. At the amateur level the international competitors are also made into warriors—soldiers who must prove the strength and nobility of their country by winning.

All these factors are exerting tremendous pressures on the athletes and driving many to the misuse of the winning-edge drugs and to the abuse of the recreational drugs. Added to these pressures are those that dedicated athletes impose on themselves—the pressures to always perform at their best and to prove themselves champions.

As so many athletes and fans now see it, these pressures must somehow be reversed. Perhaps, with all the money involved, it may be too late to reverse those at the professional level. But there is a strong feeling that much can be done at the amateur level and that everyone can lend a hand. Sensible people can demand that the politics be taken out of international competitions. Sensible parents and friends can teach the very young that sports are for fun, that winning isn't everything, that a Little Leaguer needn't perform like an adult professional, and that good sportsmanship and graciousness in defeat are characteristics that have been admired everywhere throughout history. As they grow older, athletes can be urged to see that, while they'll always want to do their best, there is no real victory when it is won at the risk of a health ruined through drugs.

Perhaps if we all can learn and communicate these lessons, sports will be able to go on being what they were always intended to be—healthful, exciting, and happy contests of skill and prowess.

What do you think? And what do you think you can do to help?

# SOURCE NOTES

——

The following source notes pertain only to the material that has been added to the book for this revised edition.

### CHAPTER 1
### Going for the Winning Edge

**1.** C. W. Nevius, "The Surprise Is That Johnson Was Caught," *San Francisco Chronicle*, September 28, 1988.
**2.** "High School Teens Admit Steroid Use," *San Francisco Examiner*, October 28, 1988.

### CHAPTER 2
### Anabolic Steroids: A Health Menace

**1.** D. Dietz, "Officials Say Illegal Sale of Steroids Is Common," *San Francisco Chronicle*, September 28, 1988.
**2.** Ibid.
**3.** The material about Ben Johnson's disqualification and loss of his gold medal at the 1988 Olympics is developed from H. H. Denton, "Johnson Goes Home in Disgrace," *Washington Post*, September 28, 1988; R. Dolphin, "Sabotage at Seoul," *Ma-*

clean's, March 20, 1989, 47; T. Gup, "Running Again—On Empty," *Time*, January 21, 1991, 72; E. Marshall, "The Drug of Champions," *Science*, October 14, 1988, 183–184; "Johnson Stripped of Gold," *San Francisco Chronicle* (from *Washington Post*), September 27, 1988; "Drug Use by Olympic Athletes," *San Francisco Chronicle*, September 27, 1988; *The World Almanac and Book of Facts, 1990*, Newspaper Enterprise Association, 1989, 861; "Ben Johnson Returns, Finishes 2nd," *San Francisco Chronicle* (from Associated Press), January 12, 1991.

**4.** Marshall, 183–184.

**5.** Denton.

**6.** Marshall, 184.

**7.** Gup; C. Neff, "Hooked" (from "Scoreboard"), *Sports Illustrated*, September 24, 1990, 27; "High School Teens Admit Steroid Use," *San Francisco Examiner*, October 28, 1988.

**8.** V. S. Cowart, "Blunting 'Steroid Epidemic' Requires Alternatives, Innovative Education," *JAMA: The Journal of the American Medical Association*, October 3, 1990, 1041; "Teen-Age Steroid Use Surveyed," *Facts on File*, September 14, 1990, 684.

**9.** Neff, 27.

**10.** Cowart, 1041.

**11.** Ibid.

## CHAPTER 3
### Anabolic Steroids: Broken Bodies, Troubled Minds

**1.** E. Marshall, "The Drug of Champions," *Science*, October 14, 1988, 184; "High School Teens Admit Steroid Use," *San Francisco Examiner*, October 28, 1988.

**2.** The material on the dangers of physical injury in steroid use is developed from: C. W. Nevius, "The Real Surprise Is That Johnson Was Caught," *San Francisco Chronicle*, September 27, 1988; "Johnson Stripped of Gold," *San Francisco Chronicle* (from *Washington Post*), September 27, 1988.

**3.** "Drug Use by Olympic Athletes," *San Francisco Chronicle*, September 27, 1988.

**4.** J. Izenberg, "Another Lesson in Perils of Steroids." *New York Post*, July 1, 1991.

**5.** The material on the possible link between steroid use and psychotic behavior is developed from: L. Goldberg, "Steroids Cited in Legal Case," *San Francisco Examiner*, October 23, 1988; Marshall, 184.

### CHAPTER 4
### Anabolic Steroids: Why Athletes Risk Them

**1.** S. Bressan, "Doping for the Competitive Edge," *World Press Review*, June 1989, 59; D. Dietz, "Officials Say Illegal Sale of Steroids Is Common," *San Francisco Chronicle*, September 28, 1988.

**2.** "High School Teens Admit Steroid Use," *San Francisco Examiner*, October 23, 1988.

### CHAPTER 6
### The Amphetamines in Sports

**1.** B. Lorge, "The Pressure Is On to Pop," *Washington Post*, May 28, 1979.

**2.** V. S. Cowart, "Blunting 'Steroid Epidemic' Requires Alternatives, Innovative Education," *JAMA, The Journal of the American Medical Association*, October 3, 1990, 1041.

### CHAPTER 7
### Braking and Boosting

**1.** The material on EPO is developed from: L. Jereski, "It Gives Athletes A Boost—Maybe Too Much," *Business Week*, December 11, 1989, 123.

### CHAPTER 8
### Cocaine: The Drug of the 1980s and 1990s

**1.** *The 1990 Information Please Almanac*, Houghton Mifflin, 1990, 102.

**2.** "Ex-Padre Alan Wiggins Dies at 32 in Los Angeles," *San Francisco Chronicle*, January 16, 1991.

**3.** D. Anderson, "The Year in Sports: 1989. Shocks, Aftershocks and Heroics," *New York Times*, December 31, 1989; J. Durso, "Gooden Upbeat for 90s After Up-and-Down 80s," *New York Times*, January 9, 1990.

**4.** "Drugs in Baseball," *San Francisco Chronicle*, August 17, 1990.

**5.** The material on the deaths of Don Rogers and David Croudip is developed from: W. C. Rhoden, "Death of an N.F.L. Player: Questions Persist," *New York Times*, October 22, 1988; "NFL Player Dies, Cocaine Suspected," *San Francisco Chronicle* (from *New York Times*), October 11, 1988.

**6.** B. Reynolds, "Marvin Barnes Leaves Jail and Drugs Behind Him," *San Francisco Examiner* (from *Providence Journal*), November 11, 1990.

**7.** Rhoden.

**8.** The material on testing for cocaine in the National Football League is developed from: R. Demak and J. Kirshenbaum, "The NFL Fails Its Drug Test," *Sports Illustrated*, July 10, 1989, 38, 40.

**9.** The material on the use of cocaine and crack among college and high school students is developed from: *The 1990 Information Please Almanac*, 102; *The World Almanac and Book of Facts: 1990*, Newspaper Enterprise Association, 1989, 171.

**10.** E. Almond and L. White, "Drug-Testing Fraud Rampant at USC," *San Francisco Chronicle* (from *Los Angeles Times*), February 4, 1991.

### CHAPTER 10
### Marijuana

**1.** *The World Almanac and Book of Facts: 1990*, Newspaper Enterprise Association, 1989, 171.

**2.** The material on the suspension of Rick Leach is developed from: C. W. Nevius, "Leach Suspended: Drug Use," *San Francisco Chronicle*, August 17, 1990; G. Shirk, "Positive Test Triggers Giant's 60-Day Suspension," *San Francisco Chronicle*, August 17, 1990.

**3.** The material on testing for marijuana in the National Football League is developed from: R. Demak and J. Kirshenbaum, "The NFL Fails Its Drug Test," *Sports Illustrated*, July 10, 1989, 38, 40.

**4.** The material on the use of marijuana by college and high school students is developed from: *The World Almanac and Book of Facts: 1990*, p. 171.

## CHAPTER 11
## Working to Stop the Problem

**1.** The material on the National Collegiate Athletic Association's 1990 test ruling is developed from: "Random Drug Tests Approved by NCAA," *San Francisco Chronicle* (from *New York Times*), January 11, 1990.

**2.** G. Shirk, "Positive Test Triggers Giant's 60-Day Suspension," *San Francisco Chronicle*, August 17, 1990.

**3.** R. Finn, "A Swift Punishment, A Shattered Career," *New York Times*, March 12, 1989; "He's on Ice in More Ways Than One," *San Francisco Examiner*, January 7, 1990.

**4.** J. Matheson, "The Barring of Fuhr: Is It Too Stiff?" *The Sporting News*, October 15, 1990, 50–51.

**5.** Ibid.

**6.** R. Demak and J. Kirshenbaum, "The NFL Fails Its Drug Test," *Sports Illustrated*, July 10, 1989, 40–41.

# FOR FURTHER READING

———

The following books, booklets, magazine and newspaper articles, and special materials were used in the preparation of this book in its original form and its revised edition. Most of the published works are available at local libraries and should prove of interest and value to anyone who wishes to learn more about the problems that drugs pose both inside and outside the world of sports.

## BOOKS AND BOOKLETS

American Medical Association, Department of Drugs (in cooperation with the American Society for Clinical Pharmacology and Therapeutics). *AMA Drug Evaluations*, 3rd ed. Littleton, Mass.: PSG Publishing, 1977.

Berger, G. *Drug Testing*. New York: Franklin Watts, 1987.

Drug Enforcement Administration, U.S. Department of Justice. *Drugs of Abuse*, July 1979. A publication containing articles from the magazine *Drug Enforcement*. It features articles on the nature and action of narcotics, stimulants, depressants, and marijuana.

Goldman, B., with Bush, P., and Klatz, R. *Death in the Locker Room*. South Bend, Ind.: Icarus Press, 1984.

Kruskemper, H. L. *Anabolic Steroids*. New York: Academic Press, 1969.

Mirkin, G. *The Sportsmedicine Book*. Boston: Little, Brown, 1978.

Mohun, J. *Drugs, Steroids, and Sports*. New York: Franklin Watts, 1988.

Wadler, G., and Hainline, B. *Drugs and the Athlete*. Philadelphia: F. A. Davis, 1989.

## MAGAZINE AND NEWSPAPER ARTICLES

Anderson, D. "Shocks, Aftershocks and Heroics." *New York Times*, December 31, 1989.

Axthelm, P. "Cocaine Crisis in NFL." *Newsweek*, July 25, 1983.

"Back to the Dark Ages" (included in the feature column Scorecard, edited by Jerry Kirschenbaum). *Sports Illustrated*, July 11, 1983.

"Behind Drug Crackdown in Pro Sports." *U.S. News & World Report*, August 8, 1983.

Boswell, T. "Number of 'Poppers' in Baseball Grows Fewer Each Season." *Washington Post*, May 28, 1979.

Brady D. "Rozelle Sets NFL War on Crime." *Washington Post*, June 6, 1980.

Bressan, S. "Doping for the Competitive Edge." *World Press Review*, June 1989.

Brubaker, B. "A Pipeline Full of Drugs." *Sports Illustrated*, January 21, 1985.

Cooper, D. L. "Drugs and the Athlete." *International Drug Report*, April 1978.

Cowart, V. S. "Blunting 'Steroid Epidemic' Requires Alternatives, Innovative Education." *JAMA: The Journal of the American Medical Association*, October 3, 1990.

Demak, R., and Kirshenbaum, J. "The NFL Fails Its Drug Test." *Sports Illustrated*, July 10, 1989.

Denton, H. H. "Johnson Goes Home in Disgrace." *Washington Post*, September 28, 1988.

Dietz, D. "Officials Say Illegal Sale of Steroids Is Common." *San Francisco Chronicle*, September 28, 1988.

"Drugs and Athletics." *Runners' World,* June 1983.

DuPree, D. "Basketball Players Are More Attracted to 'Recreational Use. ' " *Washington Post*, May 28, 1979.

Durso, J. "Gooden Upbeat for 90s After Up-and-Down 80s." *New York Times*, January 7, 1990.

Finn, R. "A Swift Punishment, A Shattered Career." *New York Times*, March 12, 1989.

Gup, T. "Running Again—on Empty." *Time*, January 21, 1991.

"Is This the End of Chuck Muncie's Road?" *Sports Illustrated*, September 24, 1984.

Izenberg, J. "Another Lesson in Perils of Steroids." *New York Post*, July 1, 1991.

Jereski, L. "It Gives Athletes a Boost—Maybe Too Much." *Business Week*, December 11, 1989.

Kaplan J. "Taking Steps to Solve the Drug Problem." *Sports Illustrated*, May 28, 1984.

"A Lab Discovery Not Intended for Sports." *Sports Illustrated*, January 21, 1985.

Lorge, B. "Chemical 'Edge': A Long History Behind Search." *Washington Post*, May 27, 1979.

————. "NFL Drives Pills Underground; Users Find Them." *Washington Post*, May 29, 1979.

————. "Particular Risks for Women Cited." *Washington Post*, May 27, 1979.

————. "The Pressure Is On to 'Pop'." *Washington Post*, May 28, 1979.

————, and Boswell, T. "Steroid Effects Debated While Use Proliferates." *Washington Post*, May 27, 1979.

Maisel, I. "The Stuff I Did Was Enough to Kill You." *Sports Illustrated*, May 28, 1984.

Marshall, E. "The Drug of Champions." *Science*, October 14, 1988.

Matheson, J. "The Barring of Fuhr: Is It Too Stiff?" *Sporting News*, October 15, 1990.

McNicoll, A. "The Case Against the Decriminalization of Cannabis." *International Drug Report*, October 1978.

Morga, C. "Drugs and the Athlete." *International Drug Report*, May 1978.

Nevius, C. W. "The Real Surprise Is That Johnson Was

Caught." *San Francisco Chronicle*, September 27, 1988.

Power, G. "The Drug Scene in Sports: Who, What, How and Why." *New York Times*, October 19, 1975.

Rhoden, W. C. "Death of an N.F.L. Player: Questions Persist." *New York Times*.

Rostaing, B., and Sullivan, R. "Triumphs Tainted with Blood." *Sports Illustrated*, January 21, 1985.

Shirk, G. "Positive Test Triggers Giant's 60-Day Suspension." *San Francisco Chronicle*, August 17, 1990.

Stoler, P. "The Toughest Test for Athletes." *Time*, June 25, 1984.

"Summary Report Baseball's Drug Education and Prevention Program." *International Drug Report*. May 1978.

Todd, T. "The Steroid Predicament." *Sports Illustrated*, August 1, 1983.

"Will Fines Curb the Use of Drugs in Pro Sports?" *Sporting News*, July 11, 1983.

## SPECIAL MATERIALS

These special materials were made available through the kind cooperation of the following major sports organizations.

### Major League Baseball
### Player Relations Committee

"MEMORANDUM OF AGREEMENT" (the agreement reached between the major-league baseball clubs and the Major League Baseball Players Association regarding procedures to be followed in case of player drug dependency).

### National Football League

"THE NFL AND DRUG ABUSE PREVENTION"

"NFL DRUG PROGRAM"

"IMPORTANT EVENTS IN NFL'S EFFORT TO COMBAT DRUG PROBLEMS"

"STATEMENT FROM COMMISSIONER ROZELLE"

## National Hockey League
LETTER DESCRIBING THE NHL'S ANTIDRUG POLICY

## Office of the Commissioner of Professional Baseball
"SUMMARY OF BASEBALL'S DRUG EDUCATION AND PREVENTION PRO-GRAM"

# INDEX

# ABOUT THE AUTHOR

—

Edward F. Dolan is the award-winning author of more than eighty nonfiction books for young people and adults. His work is included often in "Best Books of the Year" lists of the American Library Association, the New York Public Library, and the Child Study Association. His recent books for Franklin Watts include *Drought: The Past, Present, and Future Enemy; Nuclear Waste: The 10,000-Year Challenge* (co-authored with Margaret M. Scariano); and *MIA: Missing in Action: A Vietnam Drama*, which ALA *Booklist* starred and praised as a "fascinating and well-documented account."

Mr. Dolan lives in Novato, California.